T0162599

A CRACKED EGG

L. W. Koch

WestBow
P R E S S
A DIVISION OF THOMAS NELSON

Scripture taken from the New King James Version. Copyright 1979, 1980, 1982 by Thomas Nelson, inc. Used by permission. All rights reserved.

WestBow Press books may be ordered through booksellers or by contacting:

WestBow Press
A Division of Thomas Nelson
1663 Liberty Drive
Bloomington, IN 47403
www.westbowpress.com
1-(866) 928-1240

ISBN: 978-1-4497-9192-6 (sc)
ISBN: 978-1-4497-9193-3 (hc)
ISBN: 978-1-4497-9191-9 (e)

Library of Congress Control Number: 2013907102

Printed in the United States of America.

WestBow Press rev. date: 5/2/2013

Table of Contents

Foreword

When I moved to Perry, Oklahoma to become the Pastor of Perry Assembly of God I had the honor of meeting Larry Koch. The first time I met him he was working with a group of individuals who were attempting to overcome drug and alcohol addictions. I really didn't know how to take him; he had two prosthetic arms, with two "pinchers" for fingers. He reached out to shake my hand. I didn't know what else to do but to reach out and shake the "pinchers." It was really a life changing experience to see someone unafraid of having a disability. He had no shame, and he still has no shame.

Since this moment I have had the honor of knowing Larry and working side by side with him. His attitude is contagious! I can remember not too long ago sitting with Larry's brother in the waiting room of a hospital while Larry was having surgery. His brother shared with me that if we could just "bottle up Larry's attitude and sell it we would be rich!" This is such a true compliment of Larry. Not once has Larry let his disability be an interference for what God wants to do in his life.

As a Pastor I see people everyday dealing with low self esteem. When someone has low self esteem it affects every area of their life, and it becomes a difficult task to help them see themselves as God sees them. I believe that when people read this story it will be a life changing read and will encourage them to trust in God and know that God has made them unique, enabling them to embrace how God has made them, as the scripture says in Romans 8:31, "If God is for us, then who can be against us?"

It is my hope that Larry will come to mean as much to you as he has to me and so many others. So, I dare you go ahead, read this book and see how this amazing testimony of the Grace of God can change your life, as well.

-Brett K. Nation, Pastor of Perry Assembly of God

Introduction

When you go shopping and you buy eggs, you check the carton to see if any are cracked. If there is you remove it from the carton and replace it with a egg not cracked. Nobody seems to have a need for a cracked egg! Even though it might not be bad; but what if it is? I have felt like that egg. Though the outside is cracked, they have trouble looking past the fact not considering the truth. Fact; I'm cracked! Truth; I am made to be the Righteousness of God in Christ Jesus! All things are possible to him who believes! I can do all things through Christ (His Anointing) which strengthens me! This is the story of one who dared to ignore the facts and advise of experts who said, "go home get married and cope with what life brings your way! But he chose to live life in Christ to its fullest! This is not a religious story, but a story of faith!

Dedication

This book is dedicated to my family and friends who have helped me through this life with encouragement and love.

Also, this book is dedicated to the memories of my mother, Alice Kirtley Koch and my brother Charles who waits in heaven. And all of the prayers and Christian workers who help establish my feet on the good ground of the Solid Rock!

Great thanks and appreciation goes to my sister in law Ina Rose and Michelle, my personnel friend, who is like the daughter I never had, without whom this book would not have happened. I must mention Pastor Brett Nation and Pastor Brian Ahern and also my sister Marian who has kept me going.

The Early Days

On the day I was born the family gold fish froze to death. Big brother forgot to put a log in the fire box and it went out. Instead of putting a log in that morning, my brothers went out and played in the snow. My sister Marian stayed with Grandma Koch. Later that day dad called a neighbor who drove two miles to check on them. It snowed that day up to my brother's knees. Ahh, did I say his knees? His knees were only six inches high.

At the time, we lived at the Perry Lake, the city water supply. Later my dad, a city employee, became the caretaker at Daniel's Field, the high school athletic stadium. The family moved to Daniels Field and lived in the visitor's dressing room, which had been intended for the visiting teams. Other occupants were huge black and orange centipedes and scorpions!

Daniel's Field was built by the Civilian Conservation Corps of sandstone. The north end was the football field with stadium stands connected to the baseball field. The stands were also made of sandstone with dressing rooms at the end of the football section.

My mother would send me out to play in the morning and I went back in when my brothers and sister came home from school. It seems like the whole world was my playground and the trees and behind the out buildings were my bathroom.

I watched the Perry Maroons football team practice and run laps. One day they were not doing what Coach Daniels instructed; so they had to run laps, and I joined in and ran with them. I thought it was fun! While I was running, the coach hollered; " Look that little boy is out running you all. If he beats you back, we will be running all evening!" Needless to say, the team was not overjoyed with my running skill's. I didn't know high school kids were permitted to say or know the words they said to me; so after that I quit running and got out of the way.

One day the Blaine School football team (the Black School) came out and practiced. I remember saying something stupid, not a racial slur, and running from them. As I did my Uncle Larkin caught me by the arm and said, "Boy, they are God's children and you better respect them."(Jn. 1:12,13 NKJV)

I always listened when he spoke. My prayer young people, is that you will always have an 'Uncle Larkin to speak into your life! I've remembered that my whole life. My siblings and I were taught to give respect to all of our uncles and aunts. We were never permitted to call an aunt or uncle by his or her first name. All our parents insisted we respect all adults and address them as Mr. or Mrs. or Miss; which I did almost all the time. We were taught to honor those of age and those in authority.

I'm not sure at what age I was when my brother and sister developed polio-myelitis, I was in the second or third grade. I came down with it several days later, loosing lots of strength and energy. Gratefully it never developed into full blown polio. My aunts had us exercise our muscles by moving around in washtubs of water to maintain muscle tone, and they made us take naps.

At a later time my brother Charles became very sick. He was throwing up things I'd never seen before. My mother was very concerned, if not scared. My dad called Dr. Coldiron and he came to the stadium to see him. He found out that my twelve year old brother Charles had started wrestling and was pulling weight (forced weight loss); the coaches might of gave him something to help him lose weight. I thought the way the doctor talked Charles was going to die! I remember Dad was really angry, and I thought he was going to go whip someone. Dad declared "No more wrestling if you are required to pull weight." After that I never really wanted to wrestle.

As I growing up, I was not a pretty boy. I never really learned much about cleanliness until I discovered girls in junior high. I just never seemed to fit in until high school. Because of my birth date and taking the sixth grade twice, I could drive while in the ninth grade. I was still a loner. I didn't think school was such a good deal, so I just made it through by the skin of my teeth and with help of my senior literature teacher Rose Nisson. In fact, on my first day of first grade my dad and mother sat me between them in the car, made me get out and led me inside. Actually my dad held my hand until he got me inside. It wasn't a sign of affection; it was to keep me from running away. I was going to be a soldier. Why would I need school? And I could already count to ten by then.

I was born and raised in Perry, Oklahoma, the pride of the prairie! There was a book by that title, but I'm not sure if we were the pride of the prairie or not. On September 16, 1893, the day after the land run Perry had a population of twenty-five thousand people!' Obviously I was not born yet but I've seen pictures and there must have been fifty or so saloons. I can remember like most children, if asked, I would have said "My home town was the center of America."

It wasn't until 1956 when my oldest brother, Clarence, Jr. was graduating from high school that we bought our first television. It was a twenty-one inch black and white tube. I'm not sure how Dad afforded it, but it was day light when he brought it home, so it must have been legal. Clarence, Jr. was leaving town to go to Washington, D.C. to work with the FBI. My thought was. Ha! *I'll get to watch the TV, and he'll have to leave and not get to enjoy the TV as much as the rest of us.* In case you're wondering, yes, they already had TV there. I couldn't believe we were not referred to on the national news, and channel four, five & nine, didn't even mention us. I discovered this is a big, wonderful country. Perry, Oklahoma, is located sixty miles north of Oklahoma City on I-35, eighty-eight miles west of Tulsa on US-64, and south of Wichita, Kansas 101 miles on I-35. It's the heart of America!

Old-timers used to tell how thousands of people would come to town on the weekend because Perry was the center of the commerce in northern Oklahoma. We had an opera house, two or three theaters and maybe six grocery stores. There were almost that many when I was a child. It seemed like there was a full service filling station, on every corner. There were four drug stores with three soda fountains. I think there were three hotels, not motels, though there were some. We had cafes galore and several five and dime stores. We also had a semi-pro baseball team with their own lighted field. The Perry Oilers as I remember won semi-pro's most prestigious tournament at Wichita, Kansas. I remember my brothers shagging fouls for a dime a piece. I was too young. Every time my little legs would get me going, someone had already gotten the ball. My brother Clarence Jr, was bat boy for them. There were two major federal highways, US-64 and

US-77 and State Highway 86 and now Interstate 35. We also had a cotton gin, elevator and two grain elevators.

There were two railways running through Perry; Sante Fe and Frisco and the Rock Island. They went north, south, east, and west, with passenger trains both directions and two depots. It is still a prosperous community with potential for development. Farmers grew lots of wheat, oats, barley, alfalfa, Milo, cattle, sheep, and cotton and oil in the ground plentiful. There were two ice plants, and my dad delivered for one of them.

It's funny when I was young and saw pictures of him in uniform, I thought he was in the army. Nope, he was the "Iceman!" He grew up around Hayward Oklahoma, and drove the school bus so people called him "Bus." I always heard him called Rosie, I think it was because of his fair skin and his cheeks would turn pink at times. My brothers and I were called "Lil Rosie" for years. Some older fellows still call me that, because they never knew my given name. When I was in the service I never told anyone my nick name! Marian, my sister called me "Nature Boy" because I was so brown from being in the sun so much. I spent a lot of time at the swimming pool during the summer.

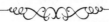

Growing Up

I n my opinion my family life was sorta shaky,. My dad worked for the city of Perry for most of our lives. Over the years he held down three or four different part time jobs. He was a shade tree carpenter, house painter, farm help, and policeman as well as others.

I think if you had asked him, he would have said, "A man has to do what a man has to do." My mother had lots of health issues, but successfully raised five wonderful kids! She had three sons and two daughters who raised successful families. I had two older brothers: Clarence, was seven years older and Charles was six years older than me. Marian, a sister was three years older than me. Nancy, the youngest, was born seven years after me. I've always said being the baby I had it made; especially the baby boy. But then Nancy came along and spoiled all that. After having me my mother had several health issues and two or three nervous breakdowns which caused the younger children to spend lots of time with aunts and uncles.

My mother had several miscarriages. She had our sister Linda Carol who died at birth at the mid-wife's office above Zorba's, which is now Three Sands Oil. Grandma Koch stayed with us and Dad said, "if I'd behave he would bring me a pair of stripped cover-alls!" When they brought mother home, I remember being so excited, at getting new cover-alls and a sister. I was a young whipper snapper and went crashing in to see my new sister. I threw back the blankets looking for her and I thought Dad was gonna kill me! Mother insisted he let it go because I was only a child. I didn't get a new sister or my cover-alls, either, Grandma said, "there just not any money to do that."

Thank God for our aunts and uncles. When my sister Nancy was born in 1951, she was the second child to be born at Perry Memorial Hospital. When Nancy was born; my mother had a terrible time. Some say the poison in her system caused her head to swell the size of a basketball. I stayed with Aunt Dorothy for a few days. Uncle Herman came and picked us up and took us to the hospital, they wouldn't let us in, so he took us to the window so we could see her. I thought mother was going to die.

I believe this was the time we stayed with Aunt Dorothy; then went to Aunt Mabel's for several weeks. Mother stayed in the hospital even after Nancy was able to come home. My aunts kept Nancy for five months. They said mother would cry for her baby. My cousin Corene at times was sent with me outside to entertain me and give my aunts a break. Thanks Corene. Dad put us on a train, (yes there was a train that stopped in Perry) sometimes I would think we had passed our stop. My sister Marian was 3yrs older than me and could read, so she would read the name of the city on the signs and tell me she thought we were not there yet. She was 8yrs old and I was 5yrs. old and she handled me just like I was her boy. Again thank God for Aunt Mabel & Uncle Herman and Aunt Dorothy & Uncle Larkin. My Aunt Viola & Uncle Mack were a big help at times. We couldn't afford a bicycle so my cousin Ruth Ellen let me use her's when I stayed there. That's where I learned to ride a bicycle and Uncle Mack taught me how to tell which shoe my foot was to go in.

Our job as kids was to help dad clean the stadium, Daniels Field and the baseball stands at the other end. For pay we got to keep all the money we found. We sometimes found whole bags of peanuts. We would return pop bottles to a service station near the stadium and use the pennies to buy candy or more pop. Since I was not in school yet, Dad would borrow from our jar. He and mother would have discussions as what to say when or if the other kids discovered it was gone.

Charles found a billfold with $40 dollars in it one day, man we'd never seen so much money at one time. We were trying to figure out how to spend it, when our aunt who was visiting said we should look in it to tell who it belonged to. Mother and I thought not, but my aunt won out. There was a driver's license, then someone said, "Call him, there has to be a big reward." Well the owner arrived and said thanks and gave Charles a dollar; a dollar, we thought what a cheap scape!! We couldn't believe it.

There were times we'd sneak out with kitchen matches; anyway I did, while picking up paper, so we could then pickup cigarette butts and smoke them. Our Uncle Phillip, mother's youngest brother, would come over and play baseball and football with us. One day as Clarence Jr. was pitching to Charles, I decided it was my turn to bat. Clarence, Jr. said I was too young, or something to that effect. I yelled to mother and she and Uncle Phillip said, "Let him bat." I stood up there with that bat and Clarence wound up and hurled a pitch that hit me in the chest. Uncle Phillip recounted at a family reunion he thought it sounded like a gun shot. He said, "I cried out; fell down, and jumped back up ready for the next pitch." I seldom got to bat, so I wasn't going to let that ruin the day.

We were country, so on Saturday morning we all went to town and went home after dark. Most times Clarence, Jr. and Charles, sometimes when dad insisted, they took me, we walked to town, we picked up pop bottles and sold them for money to spend that day. Let's see, ten cents at the Roxy Theater, five cents for a frosty root beer at Foster's Corner Drug Store! Man life never got better than that! The theater had a full feature movie, a continuing serial and cartoon.

I had a nickel left, off to McClellan's Five and Dime for a bag of candy from what seemed to me an unlimited choice! My favorite was chocolate covered peanuts! The people would walk around the square stopping to talk. At dark my mother and the younger kids would sit in the car and wave at passersby. Wow! As strange as it seems I lived for those days. The city square was four blocks square; with business on the four side of the square. There was a beautiful well manicured lawn with large pecan trees, huge elm trees, a large gold fish pond surrounding the court house with the library and post office on the corners. In those days there was no fear of child molesters or any dangers. When it was payday and dad paid the grocery store bill they would give him a candy bar for each family member!

When there was money left or if I could talk Marian, my older sister, into it she would buy me an ice cream cone. Clarence and Charles would go to Bontrager's Southside Drug to read the comics. That's where the "older" kids hung out. I never went there until I was older.

When Clarence, Jr. was 14 years old he talked mother into letting us fire off a bunch of fireworks at Shell Hill. Why we didn't stay at the stadium I'll never know. Mother could not shift so he drove us to Shell Hill, on the southeast side of town. He and Charles began shooting off the fire crackers. Well out came the repeaters. Man they were having fun, and then one went off in the grass and set a fire. Mother hollered, Clarence hollered back, "Let Larry put it out!" I was bare

11

foot and there were monster goat head stickers, I shouted "I can't!" Clarence Jr. being older and wiser said, "It will go out!" Yes it did, out of control, all of a sudden, there were several adult men shouting and sirens blowing.

We got back in the car. The men were hollering "Where are those kids that were shooting fireworks?" I was cramming fireworks behind the back seat as quick as possible and trying to hide from the men looking for us. Not sure how we got back home, but it was after dark! I remember mother was trying to explain to dad what had happened! All I know, for years I never told anyone it was us!

We moved from the Daniel's field to town when I was around 10yrs and I began delivering papers and mowing grass helping to pay my way. Dad came home one day and said he would buy me a power mower if I'd mow peoples grass to pay for it. Mother said, "NO Clarence he's to young!" I said "no I'm not!" So off to Monkey Ward, as we called it; and we got a green and white power lawn mower. I began mowing yards; one dollar, for a normal yard and two dollars, for a large yard. Funny, no matter the size of the yard everyone thought their yard was small. Don't think dad was ever happy the way I mowed, especially when he found out I charged Grandma seventy-five cents; after that the Grandma got special service. I thought she was rich. Come on, she gave me a Silver Dollar every year for my birthday, she had to be rich! (Seemed like she had a million grandkids)

I was mowing her neighbor's big yard, she thought was small, and was refilling the gas tank, when Marilyn, a beautiful classmate, walked by, oh my, I slapped that lid back on that tank and pulled that rope, and pulled that rope, and it would just back fire and blow blue smoke, she walked by and just smiled. I kicked that lawn mower, don't remember what I called it. After a bit of muttering, I discovered the kill switch was still engaged, so I quickly flipped it off and it cranked right up. Quickly I turned to see if Marilyn noticed, Nope! Marilyn was out of sight.

We were limited on what was available to eat; usually, hamburgers and pork'n beans. Dad was a cook in the Army and when we would have something special, that's what we called special suppers, dad would do the cooking. I can remember steak and fried potatoes, the good kind, cooked in Mother Tucker's Lard mixed with scrambled eggs and onions! Yes I did say, steak, they would buy one twelve ounce T-bone and divide it into six servings. If I remember right Mother's share was the bone and meat attached! Sometimes it was just baked beans and fried taters. On school days Mother would make us toast and hot cocoa for breakfast!

Dad built a rowboat; some say out of city property, ha ha, it was a good boat. We took it out to Perry Lake and tried it out! He put it in the side yard with a "for sale" sign. A well to do man came by and mother went out to talk with him, there was small talk and he looked it over a while. He asked, "How much?" Mother said, "One hundred twenty five dollars." He looked at her and shrouded his shoulders. Trying to help I injected, "oh, he said he'd take less than that!" We lost the sale, and when dad got home, I thought I might lose my life!

At about age thirteen I went to work at Stanslav's Grocery for fifteen cents an hour, if that much? Man I was rich, had over three dollars in my First Bank & Trust, savings account. I took the sixth grade over again, because I liked it so much, ha ha!

One year Mother let it be known that there would probably be no Christmas presents that year! Marian and I were talking about it, and it was mentioned my ammo box, that is where I put my money I earned from paper routes and other errands. I kept it under my parent's bed where it would be safe. We got that box and counted the money; twenty four dollars all in coins. Marian wrapped them. She and I proceeded to walk the city square and buy Christmas presents for the family. Funny, the gifts weren't what parents would buy but what kids bought for kids.

At Christmas and other special occasions; Dad would fixed our favorite candy, referred to today as, Dad's Koch Family, fudge recipe and someone would always give Dad a box of Chocolate covered cherry's. Heaven came down and glory filled the room when he would open that box! Man if anyone would have said "your family is poor," (I might have been wearing my cousin Tommy's hand me downs, old t-shirts to school, and shoes with holes, I'd called them a dirty dog liar. We would leave the Christmas tree up through News Years and I would try to get Mother to leave it up all year long. I loved the Christmas Season; still do today!

Dad was a dedicated fisherman and camper! Every summer for five years during August we went to the "River". We fished from sun up to sun down, only taking a break to swim and seine for bait. We used limb lines, trout lines, fly fishing and bait fishing on the bottom. Dad cooked breakfast, no time for lunch, and supper after dark. One morning I grabbed the first couple of flap jacks. Dad also made his own syrup (boiled water and sugar), I poured that syrup on that flap jack, ugh! Spit it out and said. "What kind of syrup is that?" Dad, "What pan did you use?" I pointed to a sauce pan, "You nut that's grease I'm going to cook the eggs and bacon and sausage in!"

At the age sixteen, I went to work for Safeway Stores Inc. In the ninth grade I was making more money than my dad. My brother and I helped with groceries and our little sister's needs. When dad left, mother would do house work or home care of "old" women at 25 cents an hour.

The actual date is fuzzy but about my sophomore year in high school, working 40 or more hours a week and going to school, there was a shift in our family's life. My dad began talking about this waitress with my mother. He began to have card parties with her and her husband; our mother was required to be involved in the games. Our family and her family began going on vacations.

Dad, being a policeman, was given a choice to end the affair or resign. He resigned and reopened the Gem Café, (he had been a cook in the Army during WW II) a small hole in the wall café that had been closed for several years. The building had two booths and six bar stools at the counter. He was told by city workers they were not to patronize the cafe. The waitress ended up leaving her job to work in my dad's cafe. He also insisted that mother work there. She did her best but she was not a waitress. So at times he had me to wait the tables, oh my, what a mistake, I wasn't a good waiter or even wanted to be there. I have done my best not to complain about a waitress since! One morning I over slept and missed my shift and he had no table help and said it was my fault that he had to close the cafe. It fell on deaf ears.

At this time I had begun to spend lots of my spare time in the pool halls. Several of us teenagers use to go haunted house hunting with mixed company. Boys and girls with flash lights in hand. We normally went to the; Old Rutherford house and the "Thrill Hill" and "Green Eyes" bridge. We would just drive the country roads; sometime we would even find parkers in what was called lover's lane. Lots of times we would stop at the Corner Lunch Cafe for coffee or cokes before we called it a night. It was a fun place with a fun waitress. We'd chew the fat for a while, sometimes we would loosen the pepper shakers lid or put a piece of napkins under the salt shakers lid and watch people dump pepper on their food or shake salt shaker trying to get salt to come out

Dad decided, as he personally told me, the "people" of Perry made it impossible for him to stay in Perry so he was going to leave with the waitress. Several class mates left notes in my desk teasing me. Dad left a lot of unpaid debts and a bank loan. I asked the banker if I would be allowed to pay them off? He replied "yes." Mother asked me not to and not to worry about it. We went on commodities, the appliance store came and got the fridge, but he said he'd give us an "old" ice box (Frigidaire) about half the size. With a married brother, in Washington D.C., my oldest sister in OKC, a brother going to school in Enid, little sister at home, I'm driving the wheels off the car, which the bank came and repossessed.

Then it was walk or talk my brother, Charles, into letting me use his car. One evening riding with a friend and his sisters we passed by this church and he said something about it, I said, "that is where I attend!" Was he ever shocked, he said "I've never seen you at church?" I had been caught! Anyway, the way Barry was I didn't think he ever went to church!

We would get a car And our high school male classmates would buy cigars; mine was a rum crook. We would roll up the windows and blow smoke until we couldn't see, then we would roll down the windows and laugh. (At what I don't know but, we had fun doing it.) We would do what we called shoot the square and drag Fir Street. We would go west on Fir street, whip through the Sonic Drive thru and drag Fir Street back to Seventh street Then "shoot" the square. Honking, waving and yelling, especially at girls. Funny how us boys would have older cars, except the rich kids, but the girls would be in their dad's or mother's car. Yes, cars, beer, and girls; yep! but we were usually respectful of others property. Most of us were taught to respect women and adults. What has happened to showing "honor?"

I was working most of the time and had to give up lots of sport activities, had to quit football and basketball and baseball, my favorite sport. Even though I hung out at some sporting events and pool halls, there wasn't a lot of close friends. There were people that called me friend. Being lonely, I started attending youth groups at church; cigarettes and all. Felt like I should do something, to make up for the family reputation, so I struggled to belong and lead. Felt inspired this is how I could prevent others from going though divorces. Myself and one girl, Frankie, as she was called, were the only seniors in the group. We had an exceptional adult leader that was a motivator. My grades were so bad, nobody, including myself, thought I could go to college, even though the Pastor thought there might be a chance. I informed my mother that I wanted to become a preacher, maybe. She laughed and said something like "no you don't." I decided to join the Marines, after all, my name sake landed with the Marines on Iwo Jima! She said "are you crazy, ask your uncle Bill, he'll tell you not to." Boys, it pays occasionally to listen to your mother.

Military Time

After graduation from high school I moved into the apartments on Ivanhoe Street. A friend of mine moved into the apartment. He was dating Connie, a friend of mine. I went to OKC for pre-draft physical. Shortly thereafter the Air Force recruiter shows up at the Safeway store. After talking to him I moved back home preparing to enter the service. I joined the United States Air Force. Jim, my friend, married Connie and got a deferment. I think, no I am sure, he got the better deal.

In the 1960's there were all these sayings like: Better dead than Red, and Hollywood's version, Better Red than dead. Some teachers had begun to say, Better to be a coward than a dead hero! Run and live to fight another day. I remember one day on a coke break at Safeway, sometimes we took them in the meat department, Hector Tovar was the Meat Manager; I said something like "Better a coward than a dead hero!" Hector pick up his butcher's knife "BOY" don't ever say that, cause cowards get their friends killed!" He sat me down waving that knife and began to tell me stories of his experiences in Korea. How his fellow soldiers turned and ran and left him and another behind; they sat back to back and held off the enemy until they could withdraw. Hector Tovar was a real American Hero. As I was leaving to go back to work he said waving that knife, "Larry don't be a coward and get your friend's killed." "Yes sir, I won't!" I replied! When I left to go to the service he had good words which ended something like, "Larry, take care of yourself boy."

One thing about Safeway we were always courteous, you know, yes mam, yes sir, no mam we have none. Once we got to San Antonio Texas, as they were yelling and hauling us around like cows. They were giving us our duffel bags which we had stuffed with our uniforms; the Training Instructor yelled "Kotch" I naturally said "Here Sir", a well trained Safeway employee. He said "now that's how you answer!" Ha ha, that was the last nice thing he said to me for weeks.

One morning as we were policing the area a training instructor walked up and handed me a 12oz bottle of Coke and said, "here, son, you want a coke," and walked off. I wanted to drink it, but something said, "Don't dummy!" I carried that coke all over the area picking up stuff. Out of the corner of my eye I spied another training instructor, walk up to the other and ask where his coke was, he pointed at me and said "he has it." Well he came storming over cussing and said, "Did you drink my coke." Those weren't his choice of words, this is a family book. I jumped up and said "SIR! NO! SIR!" I handed it to him full! I think they were playing games that morning with the "boots". He just took his coke, turned around and walked off. Always remember in those days the first and last word out of your month in basic training was "SIR!"

They told me I could choose my field of choice. After I held up my hand and said "I will" they informed me my scores were to low and because of four traffic tickets, my security level was too low to get my other choice. Well I ended up going to Greenville AFB Mississippi Trained to be a "medic". I slowly became disappointed and frustrated with the Air Force's finest over the months while stationed at Kessler AFB, Biloxi Mississippi. What a hole in the ground. The Golden Gulf Coast, dirty trashy beach, which was off limits for swimming, should have had a flusher attached! They even thought the Civil war was still being fought. They didn't recognize the Union and some places wouldn't cash US Government checks. I became frustrated with the system, volunteered for transfer to Alaska, Greenland or Vietnam. Anyway, I felt like we were in a foreign country in Mississippi.

Arrived in Vietnam April 19, 1967, my baggage had disappeared. I spent about three days being processed in borrowed clothes. They kept sending me from one table to another table, tried to get an allotment sent home and a payroll deduction. Well, as usual, it was at the next table. That night I was getting ready for bed, and mortars rounds landed somewhere and the sirens went off, men screaming and yelling. Being so far from the bunker, and no more room, I and a couple of others stood outside thinking, "it's over, come out guys." Then a squirrely Sergeant comes into the barracks screaming the civilian KP(kitchen patrol) workers weren't allowed to enter and they were looking for "volunteer" help.

The next morning they put me on a bus and sent me to town. I was not informed where I was going, so like a good troop, just enjoyed the ride. I ended up at the MAC-V headquarters compound in Saigon. Spent three days being processed there and three nights in the night club in smelly downtown Saigon, "Peril" of the Orient!!! Soon an Air Force Sgt. came and said, come with me. I got my clothes and a 38 police special and an m-16 assault rifle, and was told I was assigned to MAC-V unit in Tan An, Long An Province 40 clicks south of Saigon. I'd been led to believe I would be flying air-evac out of Vietnam. Well now I am a adviser with the 555 Military Service Flight, Milphap(**Mil**itary **P**rovincial **H**ealth **A**dvisory **P**rogram), MAC-V(**M**ilitary **A**dvisory **C**ommand—**V**ietnam). Some believe the A was for assistance! That is where I served honorably, well, most of the time. I did receive a good conduct medal.

With another Air Force airman from Oklahoma I was able to go on first aid trips with an Air Force and Navy Seabee medic. We treated anybody who came, friend or foe. Strange as it seemed, we would take one vehicle and our small arms and flack vest. If the Army should go where we went, they'd take a bunch of folks. Funny we always figured the Viet Cong were using our services, too! The big folks called that winning "hearts and minds."

We took our steel helmets off, which was a violation of orders, and wore our "RED" berets so they would know who we were! We would show up at a location and set up an aid station in a village or side of the road. Civilians and those dressed as civilians would just show up. We treated cuts, bullet wounds, shrapnel wounds and some common sicknesses. Out of the brush and banana groves, women, children and men of all ages would show up! At times I think they thought we were doctors, but they should have seen the stripes on our selves.

There was one man who came while under guard to seek aid. With no interpreter we finally figure out his problem when the guard had him to drop his pajamas. Syphilis! We gathered up all the penicillin we had and shot him until we ran out. He was instructed to find a doctor and get proper care and ordered him to have no more sexual adventures "period"! If I remember after we gave him the instructions he just smiled! Not sure if he understood the gravity of the situation of having a venereal disease and wasn't sure if the guard was because the man was a POW.

The red berets must have worked. We never lost one of us while I was there. Also served as adviser to x-ray and helped in surgery. I remember scrubbing up for surgery, the first time. The man I was relieving came in while I was scrubbing; thank goodness, I had forgot to put on my mask and surgical cap. We had a good laugh.

We did experience several attacks to our village, but it wasn't until I had left that the village was overrun but not taken. The first attack, our compound was shot at by a sniper, one round struck with in about five feet of my security position. That was one of my claims to fame. That's the first time I got to see Snoopy, a C-47 then with a Gatling gun operating.

One time two of us escorted our officers to the air strip so they could take a ride with Air Force forward air controller. After a beer, don't tell mother, we walked out to our jeep and we came under attack from mortars. At least one round hit close enough that we were hit by secondary shrapnel and dirt. I was knocked down by a fellow airman and received cuts and bruises. I was later told by my friend if I had been an officer they would of put me in for a Purple Heart and Bronze Star. After thinking about it later, it probably wasn't bad enough to get one. My army friends at home would never have let me live that down.

One time out in the boon docks an Army communications man said "Let's go to the enlisted men's club at the 3rd Div. Fire base." We went in soft caps so they would know we were "Advisers", they had fun with the Air Force dude and kept trying to get my goat. Then the sirens went off and people were hollering "incoming!" An Army specialist yelled "follow me!" Out the door we went, I wanted to jump in the ditch; he kept hollering "follow me". Looking up, I saw flashes of light coming our way. It wasn't incoming rounds, it was an Air Force F-105 taking night surveillance pictures. We followed the Army man and we ended up on the paremiter, my friend said, "What are we doing here?" The Spec 4, said, "If they attack this is where all the excitement will be!" I said something like "What in the world are we doing here!" A word of advice, follow your first impulse and jump in the ditch next time. I could not believe the well trained Army sentry couldn't tell the difference between a low flying aircraft and air burst from incoming mortar rounds.

On one occasion; on a mail run, three of us enlisted men went to Saigon to pick up supplies and take the opportunity to eat Japanese food at Mount Fuji Restaurant by the Post Exchange. After chow we were headed back to Tan An, our base, with the young Sgt. driving. We crossed a narrow place in the road, Hwy 4, and was behind an American deuce and half who was slowing for a Vietnamese bus full to over flowing with passengers. As we began to pass the truck, the bus stopped, we were just to the side of the truck as they swerved to avoid causing an international incident, and their front fender became wedged under our right front fender. The truck driver reacted and swerved back to the right. They drug us past the bus and our driver was knocked out of the jeep hanging with his foot caught under the brake or clutch pedal. He eventually got loose. The other passenger sitting in the back jumped out as the jeep steered into a rice patty. I was riding shotgun and rode it over the ditch into the patty. The jeep rolled over and landed my side down, stuck in the mud. Interestingly, it was the dry season.

My angels must been awake and on duty that day! The muddy place was the only part of the rice patty that was wet. I could hear my friends hollering that Ko-Larry, my nick name in Nam, was pinned under the vehicle! Well, yes I was pinned, but under the sandbags we had for land mine protection. I worked my way out, muddy but okay! All our weapons were caked with mud. The MP's came and were investigating when a Army vehicle from Tan An stopped. We loaded everything in their truck with the others and off they went. I stayed with the jeep. When we and the Military Police, who was investigating, had several villagers came over and tried to sell us bottles of Coke Cola. We didn't, anyway I didn't because it wasn't unusual for the enemy to put battery acid or other things like crushed up glass in Coke bottles! While standing on the side, off the road with the MP's I noticed I was unarmed. After the army dudes set the jeep up on its wheels I drove it out of the patty and headed back to Tan An.

Our unit was assigned to assist and/or advise the civilian hospital in Tan An. Most of our patients were war wounds. Like most veterans in wars before us I think the wounded children were the toughest part. One evening we were called back to the hospital. There was a little girl, maybe twelve, but was about the size of a six year old. She had received wounds and we were giving treatment in the Operating Room and she quit breathing, we worked hard to recover her but could not. That was a tough moment. We had a boy that was digging through the trash landfill the American forces used. He had a serious hand trauma from an explosion. His family who accompanied him kept telling our interpreter that a secret American weapon had injured the child. The others on duty had trouble understanding what they were talking about. I asked the interpreter, "ask them again what it looked liked." Remember, if he was injured by U.S. then we had to pay. They pull out of their pocket a device and said, "Secret American Weapon." No it wasn't. It was a blasting cap cut from a lead that was use to detonate a claymore mine. He had found it and rubbed it causing heat which caused it to detonate.

Not sure who was advising our officers, but during the Tet Offensive of 1968; we had an influx of civilian casualties.

When I got to the hospital they were assigning us guard positions. The Lieutenant sent me to the front gate and told me, "Should we come under direct attack, (it wasn't out of the question,) I was to fall back to the Central Operating Room building and we would fight from there." Pardon my lack of military courtesy, but I responded, "What, Lieutenant. If they attack I'm shooting back." Why would we allow them access inside the compound? What about the unarmed hospital employees. Now, I know they had a good reason for that defense! Well, we never had to find out and I wasn't court marshaled. They were stopped before they reached the hospital.

One evening while at the bar, did I say bar, well too late now and anyway mother is in heaven and knows every detail now, a soldier came to me and said so and so is in pain. I went to the doctor and reported the man was in pain. He said opening the safe, "Take this morphine. If he needs it give it to him. I said, "Okay sir." We went upstairs in the Army enlisted men's barracks and there he was, rolling in pain. Another Air Force medic was with me. "What's wrong man?" He replied, "My belly hurts bad. I need something for pain!" Several other Army personnel was giving him a hard time, they said, "he is in withdrawals. He is a dope head man, don't give him anything. He's coming down from a trip and he knows it." I went back to check with the doctor, he said, "If he is in pain and needs the shot, give it to him."

"Yes sir!" Went back and ask him if he thought he could make it to the Army dispensary. He thought the shot would be enough. Under protest of his fellow comrades in arms I popped him with the morphine and in about two minutes he was happy! He probably would of sang the Air Force hymn if he knew it.

Oh, I forgot, he was a security guard! It was reported that our M-60 machine gun was sold to the black market. Now, that caused a stir! They searched and threatened us with all kinds of threats. That was one of our main weapons in the compound. It could mean life or death. Some said it was traded for opium, which was readily available since they had plantations of it around us. Don't know! If it was sold or traded we knew where it would end up; in Charlies hands!

Thanksgiving, 1967, President Johnson ordered all American service men serving in the Vietnam Theater were to receive a turkey dinner. Goodness gracious we were served canned turkey loaf twice a week. We had a Army Mess Sgt., with civilian help. Thanks, Mr. President, but no thanks. I and several others ate the trimmings and filled up with C-Rations.

I was assigned to an outpost south of Tan An about fifteen clicks(about twelve miles). During the Tet offensive we were cut off from our supply and had nothing but canned chicken and turkey loaf and lima beans for two weeks; not to mention the only soft drink was lemon lime soda! During that period an artillery unit fired a round over us and it fell short, real close to us. Shots rang out and our fifty caliber opened up. Flares popped. Funny thing Charlie was sneaking by us in the dark and that round fell by them and they opened up on us thinking we knew they were there. It was a crazy war at times!

Back In Round Eye Country

When I left for the service in 1964, I said, "I'd never come back to Perry." "Yes sir, I will never come back to this place." As I was being discharged from the Air Force at Travis AFB, California, my first thoughts was don't do anything stupid, just say; yes sir, thank you sir. There were only about eight of us being discharged that day. Those idiots kept arguing with the Master Sergeant, who was in a bad mood and threatening to make us come back the next day. When I left Saigon they gave me around seven hundred dollars mustered out pay, I wasn't going to argue.

I finally got out of there, packed, and went out to catch a bus to the airport at San Francisco, to catch a flight home.

There was a cabby trying to get about five of us to share a ride. No thanks man, I've sat too close to service men long enough, I'll ride a bus with a bathroom and lots of windows. My thought, see California the best you can, Larry, there ain't nothing out here I want to see a second time! There were two or three of us at the snack bar in the airport; they must have been coming back from overseas also, because we all were trying to explain to the counter girl what we wanted. Strange, she spoke English, understood our order! I took a nap in San Fran, at American Red Cross room for service men. Got up and cleaned up, dressed and discovered my billfold was still in the pillow case. Whew! It was still there!

I flew American Airline from San Francisco to Dallas to Oklahoma City. Landed in OKC! As I was getting off and coming down the little tunnel there were shouts and cheers and people saying there he is! Man I've seen this in the movies and on TV when men returned home. Well about that time, as I'm looking for a familiar face, these words resounded in my ears, "Silly, that's not him!" That's right, correct uniform, wrong dude. My family did arrive an hour or so later. It was a great reunion.

This old war veteran spent a week just relaxing. Mother and Grandma insisted I go to church in my uniform, a decorated Vietnam veteran! Whoo Hooo! Whatever! Thank God that day came and went.

I began working for a farmer, who had ate my sisters pet chicken, and was a friend of the family. It wasn't the greatest pay, but he did have a daughter! Well, enough about that for now. My brother Charles and the Youth Minister asked me to teach Sunday School one weekend. I reluctantly agreed. I hadn't been in a bible classroom for years. Those were the most disrespectful and arrogant individuals I think I'd ever met. I probably repeated that ancient Proverb, "this generation will be the ruin of America!" In fact my Grandpa Kirtley said the same thing about me. Mother had to laugh one day when he said that, she said, "Papa said that about my age and he has said his father said the same thing about him!" We've been saying that until it has became a self fulfilling prophecy! Think it's time to change our confessions.

Driving around town in my brother's Charles' car; I felt unprotected. I had been carrying a m-16 assault rifle & 38 police special revolver everywhere for the last year. Felt naked! I bought a 30-30 lever action Marlin Golden Trigger rifle, and a '62 Chevy Impala, 2 door hard top.

I really enjoyed being a farm hand. I was out there by myself, just the tractor and me. I helped with feeding the cattle, and caring for the other livestock. This young veteran had lots to learn. I began itching for a better job with more money. I applied at the fire department and Chief said he would hire me but had to wait for approval. The department just took over the ambulance service and I was a trained combat medic and hospital corpsman, he must of thought heaven had answered his prayers. I had to do something for several weeks so went by Safeway and they hired me back. Crazy, was not the Safeway I remembered.

A city official asked me if I would go to work for the utility department as a lineman. I was excellent friends with the Utility Manager, so I said yes. Needless to say the Fire Chief shows up and wants to know why I went to work for someone else. (Wish now he'd not tarried!)

I had met a young cook who worked the same restaurant where my mother was washing dishes. Well she was nice and even attended the same church as the family. Before I got my car we would walk around Perry and went to ball games together. She started talking about college, I was talking about farming, I was still working on the farm, and she wanted to go to Edmond to school and wanted me to get a job there so we could get to know one another better. No hanky panky with this girl. At a football game I informed her I had got a real job with the city! I thought that she would say I'm committed to a home life; she must of heard, he ain't moving to Edmond, that caused our relationship to end.

By law the City was required to have regularly scheduled safety meetings put on by a Worker's Comp Safety Officer. He would talk about safety and how to care for an employee if one were to be injured. Now, it's funny, when he would ask the questions, I knew all the first aid treatment and life saving procedures. Remember, Air Force trained baby, he told them you'd better keep him, pointing at me, around because you might need him. I went out and bought me a 1969 Camaro three speed on the floor, bright yellow with a black bumble bee stripe across the hood! My intent was to buy and set up a new 3 bedroom trailer house.

My Day of Infamy

I went fishing on Sunday March 18, 1969 at the Perry Lake Park, also known as CCC Lake. Normally my choice of bait at this lake is fishing on the bottom with shrimp. On this day I chose to buy me some minnows. I baited the hook, made myself comfortable, seated on the lake bank and watched that minnow pull the cork around for a couple of hours while sipping on Colorado cool-aid smoking non-filtered Camels. Set the minnows free and went home. Told the family I got nothing, not even a skeeter bite.

That fateful day, March 19, 1969 was a nice beautiful cool day. The utility crews would meet at the power plant crew room and mechanical shop. We drank coffee, told jokes and received our work order for the day. The lead lineman and I were to install a phase of three large insulated lines from the substation, some 300 yards more or less from the power plant, which would tie into OG& E's line. I was a grunt, not a lineman, but that's what they called me. I had the hard hat, tool belt and climbing hooks. I looked like a lineman! The lead lineman told me to get into the fenced in sub-station and pass those lines over the steel I-beams while he went up the pole, some fifty feet away, to disconnect the service.

So being a good worker, I climbed up to the platform, but had trouble passing the wire connected to a large spool over the steel beam. He continued to holler at me, so I climbed up on top of the steel. He was still on the ground. Kneeling on the beam I had trouble maintaining my balance and laid on the beam astraddle the wires.

Somehow, the newspaper said "they're not sure how", but I came in contact with 13,800 volts under load carrying maybe 200 to 400 amps. Cooked me like a piece of bacon! Have you ever seen a hot dog cooker made of 2 nails with a electric cord attached? When you put a hot dog between the nails and plug in the cord and watch the dogs cook, you've probably seen how I was fried.

At the time I knew something was happening and tried to ask myself what was going on. I didn't hear any noise. Just a hummmmm, then a second jolt, I saw a bright blue sky with stars and heard this music, but not like I was used to, I thought, "Larry ole boy, I don't think that's where you were headed." Then I saw my feet floating in the air, ha! Ha!. Actually I was hanging over the glass insulators and steel beam. When Tommy, lead lineman, came running inside the sub-station where I was, yelling, "I killed you, Larry, I killed you," still conscious, I said, "No you didn't! My shirt is on fire!" I tried to slap it out, but had no use of my hands. He tried to carry me down off the beam and said "Larry I can't hold you and the beam, I'm going to drop you." I said, "Drop me Tommy I can't feel anything, I'm numb!" Well he did, an eight foot drop, thud, crack, thought my arm broke because of the loud crack I heard when I hit the rocks below. He said again, "Larry I killed you." No Tommy," I said, "No Tommy, go call an ambulance." Our radio wasn't working in the truck so he ran to the plant.

A side note was that for some reason I remained conscious through the whole thing. The second jolt came from the fact we were so close to the plant it blew out the main breaker. It turned the downtown business district and the local manufacturing plant's electricity off for thirty minutes. The power plant worker's first instinct was to throw the breaker back in, then he thought maybe someone is working on the line? That might of restarted my heart, some probably thought I didn't have one. If he did, thanks! The music was different, since then I've read Dr. Eby's book about his trip to Heaven. He and others have said they noticed the music was different and when he asked, he was told, there's no time in Heaven, so we have no beat, but a continuous stream of music without any breaks. Now I understood what I had heard, because I wasn't sure of my salvation then. I am a happy camper now!

When the ambulance came they threw me on the gurney, and off to the hospital I went. Later mother told me the Utility Superintendent met her in the lobby and told her, "Mrs. Koch we have lost Larry today!"

Now I'm in the ER with Dr. Brown and a nurse, don't think they'd ever seen a mess like me. My shirt and belt were melted to the right side of my abdomen. My leather gloves were peeled back. The thread was burned out of the leather gloves, resembling peeled bananas. My fingers looked like bacon. The electricity blew out at both elbows, under both arm pits and my lower right side. It burned black my right thigh, to the point all the ham string muscles and two of the quads were gone, and lost the motor nerve for that leg. I couldn't see these wounds till later. I kept asking them to straighten my leg, as it felt like it was bent under me, I remember saying, "Doc. Tell the nurse to straighten my leg." He put his hand under my upper back and lifted me up and said, "It is straight," and I could then see it was, I think I said "oh!" Other than that, I couldn't feel a thing.

Then next was the ambulance ride! We left Perry in a Pontiac Bonneville Hearse ambulance and was in OKC at St. Anthony Hospital in 31 minutes, approximately 65 miles. On the way to hospital I could hear the fireman, Marvin, the driver, and Joe, the attendant in the front seat talking about where we were and how Joe was car sick. When Marvin left Perry, it was said he put the pedal to the floor and it never lifted. No one is sure if that's the absolute truth. Doctor Brown had said, "Get him there as quick as possible." A nurse asked to ride with me in the back. I kept trying to look out the window to see where we were. She would pat my shoulder and say, "It is okay we are about there!" I wasn't worried about that; I just wanted to know where we were. She would say, "It's okay, honey were almost there."

On arrival at St. Anthony Hospital, I was burned 70%, 2nd & 3rd degree, some now declare it 4th degree I lost my right arm above elbow, left arm below elbow, massive muscle loss in my right thigh with nerve damage, resulting in loss of the use of right leg and severe damage to the right abdominal muscles.

After several months of hospitalization on the isolation ward a bleeding ulcer developed. The doc was more concerned with it than the burns. They referred to it as a stress ulcer. For two weeks of half & half with Maalox pumped into me by nasal tube, 24 hours a day. Sometimes visitors would come to see me for the last time, Ha! Ha! To prevent swelling they had my arms tied hanging from IV poles. Their first comment would be "how are you?" My response was "Fine thanks. I'm just hanging around!"

I believe that in all the months of hospitalization, my sense of humor was the thing that saw me through. Sometimes I would joke with them to turn the atmosphere into one of being able to enjoy the visitors. There were times of pain, skin sticking to sheets, being turned in a striker frame (we referred to it as an ironing board), muscle spasms, turning to the side and anti-biotics (big syringes with big needles), pain meds, uppers in the morning and downers in the evening and experimental drug therapy. I was so weak I couldn't lift my legs off the bed. I went from about 160 lbs to around 90 lbs. I did have a TV, which passed time. I didn't have a watch, of course, so I kept time by the TV.

They said I wasn't eating enough to help aid my body to recover. They sent a nutritionist in to see me. She wanted to know what I would eat. She had this list of foods for me to choose from, I said, "a hamburger!" She informed me that was children's food and wasn't on the adult menu. "Well you asked." The nutritionist never returned. My brother Clarence went to some drive through and got me a chili hamburger! Have you ever tried to eat a chili hamburger laying on your back as someone pokes it in your mouth? For several days thereafter everyone was trying to get me to eat. I laid in that room for weeks and never did work up an appetite.

After several surgeries; over a year's time and a long period of physical therapy, the doctor, one morning was explaining to me and the nurse how he was going to take me to surgery and fuse my knee and ankle so I could walk on it. He had her holding my leg under my knee and he said something like "He can't lift his lower leg." To our amazement, just at the suggestion to lift my leg, I did!! Very excited he said "DO

THAT AGAIN." I did, but only three times, then it was so worn out I couldn't move it again. He immediately started a extensive strength program and vitamin malts, yuck! I had to learn to walk again. I did!

After months in the hospital they began discussing the need to send me to a convalescence center to rehab. Just another name for a fancy nursing home at that time. I resisted and talked Worker's Comp into letting me move into an apartment with one nurse for days and a night nurse, for emergency, so I could train myself with her help. It was there I developed the skills of dressing, eating and being self-sufficient came to be.

Learning how to get dressed, especially putting on socks with two pairs of pliers, became a side show in itself. I think I called them every name but socks. Tying the shoe strings was short lived, but I could. Thank God for Velcro straps, now.

They sent me to Okmolgee Tech for rehabilitation! We all lived in open bay, barracks style; amputees, spinal cord injuries, mentally challenged and such! There was occupational therapy and job training. They had me go through these books of job descriptions. They said, "Larry, go through these and pick three vocations you'd like to be trained in. So I did. The counselor came back with a frown on his face and said "why did you pick these, you can't do any of these." Well my answer was, "that wasn't the instructions I received!"(Air Force trained). So he had me set through a week of auto mechanics which wasn't one of those I had picked, not sure how he thought I'd be able to change brake pads!

They had a conference and asked me what I thought, I said something like, "I'd like to go home get married and have a wonderful life." Not sure how many years of college they had, but they agree that was a good plan. They had me stay long enough to show the vocation counselor how I manage the life skills that I'd taught myself. The only bilateral upper extremity amputee they had seen was a person that the police would pick up for being drunk and trying to sell his arms in the bar to get money to buy beer. They would return him to the rehab center. So actually I was able to give them knowledge on how to use my arms so when the next person showed up, they could help some.

I started losing my balance, with one numb leg and one good leg. While at rehab I fell several times from losing my balance as I turned and the leg did not go along with the body. There has been falls since then but usually I'm the only one who knows. There have been falls where I bent the hook way out of shape, skinned the knees, banged the elbow and thumped the forehead on the ground. I do my best to land on the padded side down by spinning as I go down. They say there are less body parts to injure on the back side.

I've been known to stumble because my foot drags the sidewalk as I step. When I do that I tell the folks that

I stumbled over a rock. I have slipped on wet grass and especially snow and ice. Sometimes at night if the ground is not level or I'm not familiar with the terrain it'll throw me off and I'll stumble and if I land on the wrong leg, Katie bar the door, I will hit the ground and if I cannot get spun around to land tail gate down, with no hands to catch myself so I usually hit pretty hard.

Sometimes it's difficult for people to understand why I don't usually get out at night unless there lots of light or can park under a light. In the dark there have been times I've had to have people help me get my car keys in the key hole. If I can't see it I normally can't find it. Have you ever been in the bathroom at a building and someone leaves and turns out the light. I hope enough said.

One time I was in a old gas station bathroom and I couldn't work the door knob to get out. I just waited until someone came along and opened the door to come in, then, I acted like I was just going out. Now, if I can, I ask someone to stand by the door and if I knock, "let me out!" Especially old door knobs! Yes, ones have gotten distracted and left their post; sometimes people walking by would hear me trying to open the door and they would turn the knob! Oh! Praise God!

Before I was released by Worker's Comp and still living in Oklahoma City I would come home on the weekends. I was shopping for a car so I walked to the Chevrolet Garage to look at the new cars. Didn't see anything I wanted and asked the Sales Manager if they had any other. He said in the back building they had some they kept under cover in case of bad weather. He let me in and excused himself.

I looked around and still didn't find any that suited me. I hadn't noticed he shut the door. Well I couldn't get the knob to turn. Trapped! So I started tapping on the door then the windows. I couldn't get anyone's attention. Kenny a mechanic came over to work on a propane truck parked near the door. So I tapped a little harder and hollered. He opened the door and said, "I been hearing that tapping and wondered what it was!" The next day we were on the way back to Oklahoma City on I-35 about 4 or 5 miles south of Perry. A special news bulletin came over WKY 930 radio saying a huge explosion and fire was raging in Perry! Not thinking much of it we continued south. We could look back and see the smoke. Then they had a report from the scene that a propane truck had exploded in the Chevrolet Garage! Man, that was by the door where I was shut in! In fact, as I came out of the door I had to walk around that propane truck parked next to the doorway!

As I write this I'm amazed how many times I came close to being wiped out, but something always kept me! We all probably have the same testimony if we would take time to write our life's history!

Life Relearned

The Oklahoma Industrial court settled my case; I bought a home on a 30yr FHMA loan and bought a car. I did attempt two business enterprises. I was always interested in citizen band radios. I bought us a base and my brother a mobile. The dealer and I struck up a friendship. My other brother became a policeman so I bought an eight channel scanner from the dealer and became interested in selling them. He had bought a small building and placed it on the back of his home lot. We established our store there. I bought the stock and he was the repairman with connections enabling us to buy wholesale. I would watch the store while he worked as a city fireman.

We had some success and rented a building, calling it, The Stereo Center and added a line of four and eight track and cassette players and turn tables. Also had some console stereos and a selection of tapes and posters. We used our influence to get the utilities departments' of the city to switch from business radios to CB's and the fire department to replace their radios with less expensive business radios. During this time there was a CB war between Sears, JC Penny's, Montgomery Ward's and others. They bought them from the same wholesaler as we did, but sold them at below our wholesale price. We eventually, had to sell out. Seems everyone did get a CB or scanner in the family.

I also began a taxi service with a friend. There were two taxis in Perry then. The people discovered they could call me and say, "I'll pay you on the return trip." Then they would call the other taxi. The people were mostly older social security recipients and needed a break. Now you could ride with me and I would wait to pick them up to collect. The other demanded payment on delivery. We both went out of business!

Life was not a happy life, seems I tried everything to be happy, but only got miserable being more miserable. A new preacher came to town. My Uncle drove him by the house and my uncle declared with a booming voice that "this is where the devil lives!" as he pointed to my house. I remember thinking to myself, as he yelled it loud enough for everyone to hear and my sister was screaming to my mother what the uncle had said, "humm, that might not be that far from the truth."

With constant trying and adapting with the help of friends and family I was able to overcome most obstacles.

I was told to cope with it, by a professional adviser, but I decided I'd live with it instead. I did learn to dress and care for myself. Sometimes it's very evident that I dress myself, I can drive, mow grass, cook, write, use a computer and feed myself with some help at times. I learned early that some people need to help me more than I need the help. Forgive the word, but when they were first asking I'm would say, "I'm not handicapped, I'm just a cripple!"

I've got over it, which I should of after several years of being a snot! Now people have told others not to help, "because he can do anything he wants!" WRONG! People have the tendency to stare. That's life, get over it! The expert told me, "When people stare, just stare back!" No, that's not right. When they stare, it's at the arms, not me! The children will notice the hollow right forearm, when asked I'd tell them that's where I keep my pet mouse. Most just laugh and their curiosity is taken care of with some wanting to see the mouse.

When I was visiting my brother in Clint, Texas I liked to buy things they didn't always have. I got my niece Melinda to take me to the small grocery store there and bought fruits and nuts and food that kids and I would enjoy. We got a nice watermelon. We left the store and I got in the passenger side and Melinda got in and just sat there. I was wondering what she was waiting on, but she just kept staring out the windshield. I said something like, "What's the matter?" She said something like, "I hate her, I think I should beat her up!" "What?" "That woman is staring at you." "Oh, after twelve years I'm used to that. She doesn't mean anything by it!" Whew, she started the car and home we went. Thank you Jesus!

My home life was not normal, spent my little settlement. State legislature at that time set the amount that Worker's Compensation Insurance was required to pay. All the lawyers thought that would be a suitable amount. Charles took me to the State Capitol in Oklahoma City and the case was settled by a Oklahoma Industrial Court Judge.

I had checked with Social Security and was declared disabled. But, because of the money received from Workers Comp, I had to wait to receive anything! Thanks to Harold Sorrel and Richard Ralph they were able to build me a house at Fourteenth and Locust Street. Kenneth Coldiron, a banker and veteran, was a great help in my early years after the accident.

My mother and sister moved in with me, I would always tell people, "I do not live with my mother, my mother lives with me." We were able to help each other. As you can imagine there was lots for me to learn, everyday life skills. My instructor was life! When dressing there was how I used to do it, now a whole new way was needed to be found. From putting on socks, to buttoning shirts, tucking shirt tails, finding the zipper in the dark, toilet paper and such. Among men, that was the most asked question. I would reply, "very carefully!"

What people don't always understand, is that in the dark you see by feeling, ask any blind person. No fingers, no feeling. The results was I incorporated large or full length mirrors, night lights and always had a light available which made a lot of difference.

Now when I'd go camping, I guess I thought being a camper meant I was still a man's man! Funny how we think, I couldn't afford a camper with electric or running water, so off I would go with mother with me just in case. The others were working, so the man had to do it his way. It doesn't take long for reality to set in.

That first night came the first test when it was time to relieve oneself before bed. Oh man, it was dark, no street lights, no camp fire, could not find the zipper with two pairs of (aluminum hooks) pliers! What can I do? No, I would not, nor did I ever, ask for "mothers help" in that way.

Well, we are at the lake and people are camping and fishing around us. Ahhh ha, the solution was a flash light, a three cell metal one. It dawns on me I can really use only one arm to aim the light, the other is a helper in case you need it to assist. Hummm, I could not hold the light and unzip at the same time. I tried holding light with other hook, no good; tried finding a place to lay the light so it'd shine right. Nope, there are no counter tops at the lake. So, mother of invention, I held the three cell metal flash light in my mouth, shining down on the zipper, and was able to grasp that little piece of metal and pull. The rest I'll leave to your imagination. I always wondered what the other campers across the way thought about me wondering about with a flash light in my mouth.

I decided to run for city council and won without opposition. Served two years and retired. Did find out that I knew less than I thought I did! Also found that there were lots of people who knew everything about everything. They seemed to know when to call. At supper time! I always, as much as possible, gave them their say. I made some good decisions and bad decisions.

We had our own city garbage crews who got me more calls than anything. I had been a city employee and I knew most of the people who worked for the city or went to school with several of them. I never told anyone but I was the first council member in that period to mention a sales tax. Our expenses were out stripping our income and a huge non-budgeted expense would have broke us. I was delighted when Mayor Sheets took it up and pushed it through. It wasn't popular then and probably not today, but they all had ideas on how it should be spent. I think it should be required for every voter serve at least one term in such a position.

Before my sister got married she had bought a new car. Since Charles had left and went to Texas and married Ina

Rose, she decided we needed to drive to the El Paso area to visit Charles. We went across west Oklahoma to the Texas panhandle south then across New Mexico turning south into the boot heel of Texas to Clint, Texas. We visited lot and got to see the sites. Charles took us into old Mexico by tour bus. Nancy, mother, Charles and I saw all the normal sites, the race track and glass blowing business. When we returned to cross the border, a border agent came aboard and began asking, "Are you a naturalized citizen of The United States?" That's when it dawned on me mother had no ID with her of any kind! Border Agent to mother, "Mam are you a naturalized citizen of the United States?"

Mother blinked and said, "Huh!" My heart and soul said, "Oh No!!" Mother was dark complected and she didn't always understand why they would ask such a question. She might not even remember we were in Mexico. I spoke up, "Yes she is!" He said, "Are you." "Yes sir I am!" As you can tell we did get to cross back in the good ole USA!

A Truth Discovered

ry and try again, my life was like that a lot, I would want to do something and sometimes I would have tried and tried until it worked. Sometimes it would go on for days of trying. I use to go get coffee a lot then. Would take my own cup, that I knew wouldn't slip out of my hooks. Eventually I started asking for a Styrofoam cup. In the beginning some restaurants would charge for the Styrofoam cups.

There were times, when my humanity showed, I would become disgusted with something and just go outside or to my room and talk to it and myself. I never blamed God, that would be stupid; **He didn't tell me "GRAB THAT WIRE I'M MAD AT YOU!"** But I still had very stern talks with Him. That was before the revelation that I had "two" ears and "one" mouth, so He must a wanted us to listen twice as much as we talk! I was the first person I ever heard come to that truth. Not that I was, just the first I knew!

That was how I learned early to just "talk" to God and wait, sometimes kicked a few things! I did discover early after I recovered and was discharged from the rehab center that almost everyone reacted or responded to me as a person with a disability, because mine are visible. But I also noticed there are a lot of people with disabilities physical, mental and spiritual that can't be seen. Some people still do open the doors and offer at times to carry things for me. Sometimes I will let them help even though I normally don't need it. I said before, <u>they need</u> at times to help me more than I need the help. My friend Steven has always talked about finding the problem that caused the dysfunction. In the recovery treatment it was to find the heart issue to correct their issues. It's hard to see the heart problem if you're just concerned with a physical or mental issue.

Love and trust is the key! Not sure how many times I heard men say, I don't want to talk to him or them because I can't trust them. I wonder if God doesn't talk to us about deep things because He's not sure if He can trust us with His anointing.

When I'm with someone or a group they will ask me to do things, like, bring me that four by four, or bring that tool box over here. Hey, get the hammer out of that closet. Wheel that barrow of cement around to the other side. My response is that I can't do that, ok, I know, I can't do anything, and they usually reply something like, "Oh! Sorry man I forgot!"

To me that's one of the greatest compliments, they forgot! That to me is really cool that they forgot about my disability. Now, it's true sometimes people think or say, hey he can do anything. I've had mothers tell their children that. I remind them there lots of thing I can't do or at the risk of damaging the prosthesis, I don't. I tried to carry a ice cream in a sugar waffle cone in Braum's once. They said they didn't mind cleaning it up cause that's what we get paid to do! Or when I pull a six pack of Pepsi out of my cart to be checked out and my hook pierced the can sending pop spraying everywhere. The checker groaned, the young male sacker shouted, "Man that's the first time I've ever seen anyone put his finger through a pop can, wow, awesome!"

Before I got my first prosthesis, I taught myself with trial and error, how to light a cigarette without arms and how to write and draw with a pencil in my mouth. When I got my first prosthesis on the left arm, I couldn't wear it but a couple hours a day. Between the burn scars and those from amputation scars, the doctor was concerned I would cause sores on the stump.

Before the accident I was right handed, but since the elbow was left on the left arm, it became the primary arm of use. To my surprise, when I went to write with a pencil, it wouldn't slide on the paper. People with hands use their wrist and fingers to guide the motion of the letters formed. I had to learn to do that with my elbow which means the arm is not resting on the paper to keep it from sliding. Now I use mostly ballpoint pens with smooth flowing action and something under the paper to keep it from sliding.

My family used to love going to the Lincoln Park Zoo in Oklahoma City once a year or so. It was funny because the young children would be watching me more than the animals. You could hear them saying, "MOMMA! What happened to him, or why does he have those things." You could hear the parents' saying, "I don't know, ssshhh, shut up. Don't talk or ask about those things!" When they were close enough I would stop and show them how they worked.

One day a little six yr old girl asked, and I said, "I got burnt and they gave me these to use." She said, "What happened to your hands?" "The doctor had to take them off," her reply "you tell the doctor not to do that anymore!" My response to such inquiries are that God didn't do this but Jesus takes good care and helps me, ah, where do you go to church? The parents have to answer that one!

Rev. Robbie Work became a friend, pastor, and mentor. Robbie was the pastor riding with my uncle who pointed to my house while my sister was in the yard and heard him say "this is where the devil lives!" As I said, "he might of been close to right," ha! Ha! A week or so later my uncle brought Robbie by for a pastoral visit. We exchanged the usual greetings. Robbie "Have I seen you in church since I've arrived?" Nancy, "Oh! I have to stay home and take care of

Larry in case he needs something." Mother said, "Yes, same for me." Me, "No, I just don't go and you all can go anytime you want. Don't blame me."

Robbie was very polite, was a big man about 6-4 and bald. I believe after our visit I said I would "try" to make it some Sunday. After all the people said he had a dry personality and a boring delivery. In other words, no jokes or pretty poems. And it was rumored he "spoke in tongues", but our Grandpa did that, and the messages were longer than 20 minutes. The board took care of that. You would of thought they were talking about heresy and blasphemy! No jokes, poems or a smile, just the word preached with conviction. I did sneak in a couple times and to this day don't understand what their problem was. I got home and the question, "What did you think?" "The man's a teacher, he speaks different than most preachers I've heard, but very sincere, and I think he did smile a couple times."

The Girls and God

One interesting day my sister called me from the bank and said that there was a woman in her drive thru teller line saying they were looking for softball coaches for young girls. She told her I would coach, then called me and asked and informed me at the same time she told them I would. I replied, "How can I coach! I can't even throw a ball," she said, "That's okay Larry, I will help you!" OH! That's real comforting, I thought, she had never played!

We met with the league commissioner she said, "and the other team," "other team", ah what, well since they'd played together the year before on a special made up team she was going to assign them as a team and I could have the rest. No, rules say teams will be drawn. They had already made slips of paper cut with scissors of that team. The other girls were on a sheet of paper. They tore the names from the paper which gave their slips a rough edge. It was decided since I couldn't always grasp one slip at a time, someone would draw for me.

Would you believe every slip drawn for me had a rough edge except, one and every slip the other coach drew out had a smooth edge? Every player on my team except for three had never played organized ball. Wonder how that happened. Then we drew for sponsors, I drew the one that had bought Maroon shirts.

It looked like things were looking up, then the phone, ring, ring, the league President, my brother, calls, the sponsor with the maroon shirts wanted the other team to have their jerseys if they were to sponsor, wonder how that happened! I said, "That's okay we will beat them with black shirts advertising a funeral home." Each team started with eighteen or so players, our team had eighteen players who played every game. The other team dropped to thirteen or so. We had a good building year and were very successful the next year.

One of my real joys was playing all the girls and letting them all start a game. The third team I coached we were playing for the League Tournament at the end of the season. I started a girl at second base who had not started a game yet. She came to me crying saying we were going to loose because I was starting her. I could hear the parents saying the same thing to the assistant coach loud enough for me to hear! I told her, "if I thought she couldn't do the job I wouldn't play her". Also I said a prayer, "Oh God help us!" The first batter hit a ground ball to second! She fielded it and awkwardly threw the runner out. The team erupted in cheers.

After she had got to bat I replaced her with a girl who if playing on any other team would get to play only if they were ahead by fifty probably. With two out, top of last inning a ground ball hit to short stop, she threw it to second, I might of sucked air, but the second base player caught the ball, stepped on second base and put out the chance of the other team and we won. Those girls never got to play again, but they have a story to tell their daughters and granddaughters! Pardon me if I smile thinking of the look on their faces when they made those plays and the cheers of their team mates!

During that first year there were a couple of girls who were different, not strange, they laughed and joked and played like the others. I began to hear them talking about church like it was fun, strange thing I knew where they were going to church. Kept listening and they talked about singing and bible study and they were happy. They were not rich or from a upper class society, but they were happy. Now as it so happened that's what I'd been looking for. Most of the others were mad or talking about boys or how they wished things would be different.

Then God, good ole God, sneaked up on me. A person came to practice one evening and said, "would you serve as a deacon." My reply, "what, you better find someone who deserves it." The person said, "We think you are that one Larry, we need you." "Well if you can't find any one," I figured out of a church with a roll of 640 or so with 350 active, I was off the hook, there had to be someone more deserving. Ring ring, hello "Larry this is Don and we are having a new deacon's meeting!" Against my will I went, there were two plus Don, Don said one of you is our new Chairman of the Deacon. All I know, Mike, the other said "fat chance." Guess who that left? That is right! God sneaked up on me again! Oh, those girls, one became my brother's daughter and the other his daughter in law.

I even began attending Sunday evening service. Couldn't believe the attendance was so low. But, the Word was taught, not church doctrine, and we got to choose the songs we sang. I had really found a peace in my heart that I couldn't explain. The next thing was the need for learning and being a part of this new experience.

That Sunday I noticed in the bulletin several Bible studies. I chose to attend the study at the O'Dell's residence since Mr. O'Dell and I had developed a friendship. It said Bible Study 10am. Well, being I didn't want to be late and get a good seat I got there fifteen minutes early. Now they only lived four blocks up the street, but Faye O'Dell was well known in the state and after all a church that large you ought to arrive early.

Arrived as planned and first thought, check the bulletin must be wrong day or house. Finally decided which house I would ring the bell on, yes it was the right house, Mary answered the door. I said, "This is where the Bible study is going to be." Yes she said, "You're early, but come in." I mean I thought at least thirty or forty folks would be there. Let's see, me, Meredith, Robbie and Mary Elizabeth and Faye and of course Mary.

They began with prayer, and Meredith was so sincere and rocking a little and praying or something when Robbie open with prayer, I thought man now I know what it means, "fox in the hen house." Robbie then read scripture and they discussed it. To my surprise Moses wasn't Abraham's dad and Jacob was Joseph's dad, but how did Mary's husband get there. I had seen the Ten Commandments movie, but someone was all messed up, yes sir, it was me! I went home enlightened and a little embarrassed, that day I decided to read the Bible to learn; not just to do it because that is what Believer's do!

It seemed, I couldn't understand it but the knowledge who to listen to seemed to be with me where ever I went. Today I understand, as I would walk in the door where ever someone was teaching or preaching and I knew, I just knew who to receive from and who to let it pass by without receiving it! It was amazing how many of people since have told me the same thing.

One night at a revival, A Methodist preacher gifted in the things of the Spirit, which he never mentioned, but we had large crowds because lot's of Methodist from the small towns came. Shouting Methodist, they called themselves.

While praying before the service started and then again during, God spoke and said, "Lay hands on the sick and they **will recover!**"(MK16:18b NKJV) I knew that was in Mark 16. It took some time, between God and Robbie, to understand that "hooks" would do.

I am a little hard headed at times. I was probably a Christian in name mostly. I might of missed Heaven by eighteen inches if I'd croaked then. Eighteen inches is the distance from your head to your heart! Lots of people would cuss(my word) Christian TV, but I learn several important Biblical Truths. One important thing about me was I never learned many religious things, so I didn't have many to unlearn.

John chapters 14, 15, 16, 17; I learn He, The Spirit of God, the Spirit of Truth would lead me into half the truth, NO, He said "ALL" the truth. And show me things to come. Things to come, then they would say, "man that's of the devil and nothing but emotions," Hey it's in the RED. Oh brother that's not for today and you're certainly not an Apostle that walked with Jesus. He said He spoke not only to these but for those who heard and believed their teaching of the Word. And Jesus would give to them what His Father gave to Him and would show and or give them to us. And remind us of the things He told His Disciples. We were told the, truth shall set you free. Yes that's true, but I heard school teachers, politicians and drunks at the bar proclaiming that. I checked it out. "If, My word abides in you and you Abide in Me, then you will know the Truth and the Truth shall make you free."(Jn8:31,32 NKJV) He and His Word abide in me, man no wonder I could not understand the Bible when I read it. Nothing in me except junk, you know junk in, junk out, but when I yielded to the Spirit of Truth for my information, and dumped the junk, there was a lot of room in my heart for Him and His Word! In the spirit it must a sounded like a giant vacuum sweeper taking in Wisdom and Understanding.

I complained to God once or twice that nobody taught me what I need to know and was I angry with them. I heard a soft quiet voice say, _**"Larry it's in the Book!"**_ I was amused and tickled with that answer and began to laugh out load. "Yep, God You are right, all I had to do was read the book. No one to blame but me!" My Angel was probably dancing and swirling around shouting. Oh, yes there are still people who think I'm too Godly minded to be any earthly good.

There are people who say, they never felt condemned by me but were always encouraged when I left. I like the latter! Anymore, living alone and spending most of my time alone, even in a crowd, when someone comes by the apartment or at coffee shop and asks a question, sometime they just sit down, I explode with things of God or His Word or thoughts I've had, and begin to chatter like I've never seen anyone in a million years. Just ask my friend who comes by twice a month to clean!

In early years after I really got saved I heard a teacher say if you are young in the Lord; he would give this advice. You should only have a few maybe five at the most friends who are believers and then after you've become efficient in what you believe, not doctrine of men, but the Word of God, you should have one good friend that's a believer and four that are unbelievers; so you can be a testimony and witness to what God has done in your life. Now the purpose is not to backslide, but be a witness.

In the beginning I used to be concerned that I would be misled into head knowledge teaching. So I asked the Holy Spirit, as much as I knew of Him, after all that's all He really expects from us is as much as we know of Him and His Word. That was before I discovered that Jesus said He would send us the Spirit of Truth, Who would lead us into all truth!(Jn16:13NKJV)

Good time to chase a rabbit! One Sunday morning, Mr. Hall teaching on the Holy Spirit, I began to get upset because the adult students kept asking why we need this Spirit stuff. Strange as it seems that's all they had ever heard. Almost only time we heard it was at baptisms and singing the Doxology! After all He hadn't been around for years and we were doing okay without Him.

I left there so mad, went to the church after lunch to pray, God told me we were teaching strong word, meat as Paul called it, and they were choking over it. So I decided to love them anyway.

During times like this, Larry Hall, the teacher, would tell us a story, this one is one of my favorite. There once was a little boy who was poor and always wanted a new ball cap. One day his dad brought him a new cap, "red" I imagine, so he proudly wore it outside so everyone could see his new cap. One day the wind blew his cap off and it landed on the other side of a fence. He couldn't get to it. The fence was too high and the gate locked. Standing there looking at his cap broken hearted, tears flowing; he began to say his ABC's. A man happened by and said, "Son what's wrong!" The boy said, "The wind blew my new cap over the fence and I can't get it!" At that, the man stepped over the fence and retrieved the cap. As he gave it to the boy he asked, "Why were you saying your ABC's?" The boy responded, "I didn't know what to pray so I said the ABC's and let God put them together!"

I had gone to Broken Arrow to see Charlie and Ina Rose for a visit. Had a good visit and impressed with the growth that the Holy Spirit was providing their family. I am not one for driving around at night, left early enough to arrive back home before dark. When I topped the hill east of Perry, the Lord began to talk, not audible, but I did answer with thoughts. He said buy the building and start a church! I said something like, well maybe the small building but not the large one. He said the large, my response was I do not know anyone who thinks I am a preacher, why not call Charles and Ina Rose? The conversation stopped there.

I was not sure what to do so I let it slip on by. Couple of young adults in a bible study told me they had been calling out Charles and Ina Rose by name asking God to send them to Perry. I had started a Christian Book store with my sister as the manager. I had kept my ODOT job and used a loan from a local bank. That was a interesting time of prayers and frustration. Nancy moved back home and lived with mother and me and received room and board and her car payment paid!

Then Nancy went and got married, and left us her dog with eight puppies and her cat! At that, the store was closed. I did have the honor to pay for her wedding and walk her down the aisle!

Change Cometh

This time was a time of trial and examination of my beliefs and life style. There was a group of folks coming to the Church called, Lay Witness Team, well I did not want anything to do with them thar Holy Joe's. I had planned not to attend. My brother Charles and I had began going to a bible study group, another page somewhere for that experience, and the change in my life had begun to be evident to some. One day I was spouting off to the church secretary and told her, "I am glad these people are beginning to change and behave more like they should." Her reply, "No, Larry, you are the one that has changed!" That took me by surprise and shock! The Pastor asked me to give my testimony two weeks before the Lay Witness Team was to come. I shocked myself and everybody by what came out of my mouth. Then he assigned me to be with the team that was coming.

When talking about me I would usually introduce myself like, Hi! I'm Charlie Koch's brother or Mrs. Kirtley's

Grandson, or Larkin Kirtley's nephew. I had no confidence or idea who I was, so why would anybody else know who I was.

I certainly did not know anything about who I was in Christ. Well I was a hit, ha. ha. So I traveled with that team and a similar Charismatic team for several years. I drug several adults and lots of young people to different cities and states. Our team leader, Hugh Harrison, had a saying, "If you knew how little attention people paid to what you do, you would be disappointed."

I had met a man who became a close friend. He would recall after he started to attend church that they would pray the Lord's Prayer. One Sunday as he was praying "forgive me as I forgive others," he realized he had not forgiven them! He went to the Pastor and demanded to know why he had him asking God to forgive him as he forgave others. "You have had me asking God to forgive me as I forgiven others, I have not forgiven anyone nor did I intend too. Now why would you have me do that!"

I remember when I would pray that part Thy Kingdom come; thinking all the time, "God not yet, I want to have a wife and family and 12 girls before You come!" We had a wonderful Sunday School Teacher who did not have any problems with me. He taught me a lot about the Word of God and the Holy Spirit. He had a quote he would say when you acted like you were the smart one. It went something like this: <u>"He who toots his own horn, will find out nobody will give a toot!" Hezekiah 3:3</u>

I could not sleep without having weird dreams and images in my mind. I was having trouble sleeping at night while attempting to receive the baptism of the Spirit. In my earlier years a boy we never said anything like I love you, especially to a male. In fact if I had said that and tried to kiss my dad, I would of found myself on the floor. Now I had never seen God, so it was easy for me to say "I love God." Never would of even talked about the Holy Spirit, but Jesus, He is a **"MAN"** and there was this block. After two years of trying and hardly no sleep, finally relief, spelled "Peace." For two nights in a row I was awakened dreaming of laying hands on the sick praying in the Spirit!

Funny, it still took a trip to Clint, Texas to visit my brother and his family! We were called to a man's home dying of cancer. We prayed for several minutes, the room filled with a mist. Man I thought, "It is going to rain". Then I noticed the sun was shining bright outside. The mist even seemed to be a little ways outside the room. That is when it happened. Yep, God proved everyone wrong in my mind that day! Well, there were no lighting strikes, peals of thunder or roman candles! Nope, just a new way to pray! Charles' daughter was the only other one who saw the mist, and mentioned it. I was not going to say anything. Man! God did really exciting things back in those days. A side note is He still does today.

Now I had to revise all my teaching on tongues. I was the doubter's best advocate, now their worst nightmare! Praying in the Spirit opens the door to the Supernatural! When the thought; God does not do that anymore. Don't you know healing is a thing of the past, we have Doctors and hospitals, amen, I'm happy for them, especially in 1969 and 2012 and many times thereafter, but, then I began to see God do supernatural things in people's life!

What was the difference, the Word of God came alive, because He is Alive. Praying all kinds of prayer and praying the Word open the door of Faith. Whew, now do not close the door.

The University of Pennsylvania set out to disprove this gift of speaking in an unlearned language. Not being there I can only report what I have read and heard. They hooked up probes to the brains of people who claimed to have that gift, to monitor the area of the brain that controls speech.

When they began speaking in that language that area of the brain went quiet with no activity. The people said that the language came from the heart of man, the spirit. Romans 8 tell us we are praying with the help of the Spirit Who knows the mind of God, and He prays the will of God.

Now, if you ask me now, if I want to pray the will of God or just some sort of popcorn prayer, at one time I would of said, "that's scary, not me," but now, I want and need to know the mind and will of God, cause there are many times

I don't know what or how to pray and I would rather pray the will of God in those matters not the doctrine of unbelieving men! Rn8:26,27NKJV) I know that's strong and comes from a man considered uneducated!

Since attending the O'Dell's Bible study I was looking for a Bible Study group to attend. Charles had bought me a book to read; well I was really confused after that. I started reading four different translation of the Bible. I had watched some Christian programs on TV. We did not have cable at that time so we were limited on the programs.

Charles and I went to Church one Wednesday evening and sit like the third row from the back. Two women coming in after us sit in front of us. We exchanged greetings and polite talk. Then one turned around and said, "Why don't you come to our bible study on Thursday evenings here at the church." The other women spoke quickly and said, "No, you wouldn't want to. It's not for men!" I said, "Sure we would!" That second woman became Charles' wife several years later.

It was a prayer and share group for divorces. I think we were considered confirmed bachelors at the time, and she did not think single men at a divorce's bible study would go over well. We went anyway and the Spirit grew all of us into a strong group of prayers and committed to the study of the Word and discovering what God had planned for our lives. Ina has been a mentor and encourager in my Christian walk and precious sister in the Lord as well as a supportive sister-in-law. While attending that prayer and share group we listened to cassette teaching tapes of several different teachers. Every once in awhile me or someone would shout, "hold it, stop, replay that again!" I have never heard of some of those teachings. They were all found in the bible. I was like a sponge in those days.

Larry a man, who had run from church, could not get enough. That's when the local church got me to be a deacon, and almost immediately put me in charge, was not difficult, it just required someone who would be committed to planning and arrangement of serving deacons every Sunday!

Three years later I was nominated as an elder. After a couple years went by I was elected Chairman of the Board. Who becomes President of the Elders. It was a time of growth and experience of growing a church. There had been times when I wanted to rap the gavel and say, "This is how it's going to be," but, God taught me not to Lord it over "His" flock and be an encourager of the people to discover their gifts and assignment from God through the Holy Ghost to fulfill their place in the local and the universal body of Christ.

Maybe the most difficult thing was getting the congregates to understand warming a pew was not the gift they had been entrusted with. After all, they were just hearing that they had been given a gift, Romans 12. I believe they thought when they hired the pastor/minister he was supposed to do those things, after all they were paying him for doing something more than one hour on Sunday and Wednesday.

One time in 1980, Pastor Work asked me if I would go to the City with him for a Pentecost 80 convention. He said that a man, do not remember his name, but had been dubbed "Mr. Pentecost" was to be the main speaker.

We had several different classes we could attend. We chose the class on "Healing in the Church Today" taught by a nationally known Catholic priest who ministered in the area of healing. Pastor Work asked me what I thought of the teaching when it was over. I enjoyed it and it revealed some things I had questioned. When we turned around to leave there was a man I knew from the Pentecostal church in Perry. He worked at the same place I did, so making conversation, I asked him what he thought. He replied, "If I could have understood what he was talking about it'd helped?" Huh! I looked at Pastor Work and he looked at me.

Later I remembered saying "How could a Pentecostal church leader not understand?" He just shrugged his shoulders! Must have been offended by the speaker's collar! Remembering Numbers 22:22; I was not going to let the church and dress of a man keep me from hearing from God. No donkeys for me! There was a time I might have been one, but that did not mean I need one to speak to me!

We began to have two Sunday morning services, first was the contemporary and the second was the traditional service. The first service we had the young people of the church led worship and presented the word. Pastor Work preached the second service. We had a guitar player lead Worship sometimes with a trombone player. We also used an overhead projector and screen to sing from.

We had been having them for about a year when on Easter an older elder came in and wanted to know what was happening. I informed him that this was how the 8:30 service always was. He replied, "A guitar!" My friend is coming and he will not like the guitar!" I said, "He would be mad over a guitar!" The man said "Yes! That's why he's coming here this morning because they are having that music where he is going! And I want him to come here and I told him we do not do that here!" But, that's what we did at the early service! There was a nice crowd that early service and some of the congregates were surprised by the music, but none complained that I heard. Not sure if the elder's friend came or not but the elder's family including his daughter and granddaughter who "danced standing on the pew" enjoyed the music.

At work seated at my desk several people would drop by to just talk. One day it was slow and a person assigned to our Division though he worked for another division would come in to hang around. It seems like at times he thought he was my supervisor! He would talk about country churches with loud music that he made fun of. I said, "Jim where do you go to church." Jim, "Oh I don't go, pardon the reason but Sunday is my day to rest and I sleep in." I responded, "My day to sleep in too, Jim. I get up about 8am on Sundays. Which is three hours later than normal."

Training Years

I n those years I would get up around 5am, never set an alarm, I let the Spirit wake me. I heard an internationally know preacher teach that's one way we can trained our self to hear from God and pray in the Spirit until release, read six chapters of the Bible a day. Next meditate on the day and be at work ten minutes early! My dad trained us boys always be early!

In the evenings after supper it was one hour of cassette tapes of bible instruction. Then read and study scriptures for one hour and then pray over prayer request of mine and others given to me during the week. I would at times pray over the world map as led.

Now, that sounds like a lot. But the folks I went to church with, that was a small amount of time spent with God! Upon arriving at home one day my mother met me with these words, "I lost my glasses." "Where did you last know you had them?" She replied, "The back yard. The dog jumped on me and knocked them off." Now I went out and could not find them,

I went back in and thought how in the world were we going to replace them. Then came a thought, walk the whole yard, they are there! That is what I did, started walking a circle until they were found. Another time I'd come home and there would be several flies and the house was very warm. Couldn't figure out where these flies are coming from and why all the bread was always gone.

Well, one morning I forgot something so on my coffee break I went home. When I walked through the door, the dog greeted me, seems mother would get lonely and open the door so the dog could run in and out. When she would see me or someone coming she would throw the bread into the garage so the dog would run out after it and then she would shut the door as nothing was up. I solved that problem!

I have told people that I'm like a 55 Chevy, in good shape, with some missing parts, but I'm still a classic! While still at that church, a man who attended the same church asked me if I would consider going back to work. Strange as it seems I had tried with a manufacturing company to get a job and was told they had nothing I could do. Gene said, "Won't the church hire you to do something?" I replied, "ahh no sir!" His reply, "Well, if I don't call you in a couple weeks, call me!"

It was not long after that Bob asked me, "Why don't you come out and see me about a job I think you would be good at?" I was excited that he wanted me and had a plan of employment for me already. Bless Bob Stringer's heart. I saw him enter a café, so I hustled in and spoke with him again just to make sure he was serious. He said he was, so I hurried right out and filled out an application and talked to Bill my, unknown to me, future supervisor.

I went to work for the State of Oklahoma, fifteen years with the Oklahoma Department of Transportation in the Division Four Headquarters in Perry. It had to be a step of faith on both of theirs! They assigned me to answer the PBX and radio system. Faith, yes because they just hired a man with no hands to operate a switchboard and their communications! Thanks to Bill's patience and Wally the SWBT man, I was finally able to conquer that switchboard, PBX, and get a hang of the Division wide communication systems! Not for sure but I think several "old" highway foremen would visit Delores who was training me to see the man behind the voice. Some of them was wondering how I wrote notes that was to be taken when no one else was available.

When we moved to the new building complex I became the receptionist in the front lobby also. During this time of life I was nominated and named the Handicap Citizen of the Year for Oklahoma. I did get to know lots of people and politicians and important ODOT employees.

We were experiencing some cross frequency problems in the telephones. The repair folks would come out and do something and leave but it would always come back. Well, one day our field engineer was having a meeting with SWBT, the representative from SWBT came in dressed immaculately and had five or six well dressed men following him and saying things like yes sir, no sir, They said they would call and that kind of stuff.

I notified Manuel that his appointment was in the lobby with his body guards. Oh, my, well my sense of humor hasn't always been proper! The man said, "How do you like your PBX system?" He shouldn't of asked.

I explained my problems and he suggested we call and report it. He should not of said that, cause that's when out of my mouth came, "oh they have been here several times." About then Manuel came around the corner and led him away. As the SWBT rep left the meeting he stopped at my desk and smiled and said, "Someone will come fix it!" He shook my hook and nodded at his people and out the door they went.

The next day, two men, a local repairman and a engineer out of Dallas, I think, was standing at my desk wondering who talked to the Vice-President of Southwestern Bell? They never got that problem fixed, but we did buy a new system with fanfare from SWBT. FYI, there was nine incoming lines.

The radio system could reach almost the whole state through dial up repeater towers. I stayed after 5pm till 6pm in case anybody had a problem on the road and needed assistance. There were evenings nobody called and others when I not only helped our people, including the Director, and some people from other state agencies who had car problems or became sick and we helped them reach their destination. We had several ambulance and troopers call from accidents.

One funny time, being a techie I had a scanner listening to OHP and PD's and others. Heard a trooper call in to Perry PD, that the railroad overpass on I-35 south of Perry had moved a foot and was in danger of collapse, we had been having trouble with a joint of asphalt breaking out, the bridge had not moved, well, hearing the call I waited, Richard calls and report the problem, I asked him to have the trooper stand by there and we would have a supervisor come take a look, what I didn't tell him was after the trooper called in I heard him on the scanner go out for a break at Sooner's Corner Truck Stop. <u>Come on man, if the bridge was gonna fall down don't you think he'd stay until we got there?</u> Richard informed me that he had gone 10-45 at SCTS! I chuckling told Richard I heard the call and already reported it to a supervisor and that there was no danger of the bridge collapsing. Sometimes it was fun after 5pm!

Just remembering how things go when you think you know, but you only know what you know, well, one morning after I arrived and took my place at my desk, I heard them talking about a bridge that had been damaged. It was just south of us on hwy 86. As I listened they said only the handrails had been knocked off, but the bridge was sound. I had forgotten that when a call came about a damaged bridge, I transferred it to the Area Engineer. I decide to turn on my scanner and I heard the OHP talking about the damaged bridge, it was jumping up and down moving a foot or more.

I heard the Area Engineer ask the Maintenance Engineer if he had been notified of a bridge being damaged, he said, no. I jumped in and said it has been looked at and is in sound shape. Which he replied, okay, the Engineer ask him what bridge, he said, "on US 177", oops. I spoke up to correct myself and told him I was talking about a different bridge. Then over the scanner I heard the excited trooper explaining to dispatcher a dump truck with its bed up had struck the overhead truss of the Salt Fork River bridge. It was heavily damaged. Learned my lesson that day, don't jump in until asked! That bridge could of collapsed.

There was a woman at work who was a committed believer who always witnessed to me. The usual do's and don'ts. She would tell me what they believed and then I would tell her what I believed. Phoebe would say, "You believe that, then why don't you attend my church?" I would tell her why and she would say, "Oh Larry be careful that's could be of the devil." It's strange all those years of serving the devil he never once asked me to do any of those things. What things? You ask. Somewhere in the Bible it says, "It is a shame to discuss in the light the things done in darkness."

One Sunday I broke loose and told a group some of those things and a older lady said with great conviction and anger in her voice, "Larry, I've known you since you were a child and you never were like that!" Yes, she did. While I was speaking in Church, yes she did out loud! I called her by name, "That's because when I was doing those things you were home in bed, behind locked doors!"

The Season Changed

fter Nancy had gotten married and was pregnant with her son, in the fall of 1983, I had tried out to be a interim pastor at a local area church. Think I preached too long and was a little radical for them. I used the bible as my source for the sermon. After that week my sister said that Charles and Ina Rose were considering birthing a work here in Perry. I was still on the board of a local church and was not sure what God would have me to do. I was not an officer anymore so I meditated and prayed if I should stay or launch out in the deep with them.

After some soul searching I resigned my position with protest from some members. Left and became a charter member of Lighthouse Christian Center when my brother and sis-in-law graduated from Rhema. Charles and Ina came to see me and I informed them that I would like to be a part of their work and would join them. It came as a surprise to them. In about two weeks or so we began a home church from

Ina's sister's house. It was a contemporary charismatic service. Yes sir, all the bells and whistles and gifts in manifestation. I had joined with the intent to be a worker and not a church officer or anything likewise.

We had begun looking for a building! We had started to meet in the IOOF Lodge. One day it occurred to me to check out the building God had showed me earlier. I drove by it and it had a for sale sign on it. The smaller building, not the large one! On the building was a sign reading, "LIGHTHOUSE", by faith we began calling our selves, The Lighthouse Christian Center. It took a move by God and financial favor of a member, but several weeks later we had signed a lease purchase agreement to buy the building.

After we began to incorporate they asked me to be a trustee. After some convincing I agreed. Several months later a youth group from a neighboring community church came to visit our services, my thought they have come to see the nuts! Found out later the youth leader was a Spirit filled believer. I think I was hoping everyone would behave and not have any Pentecostal outburst, sorta speak. We were full so I'm sitting on the front row, the Praise and Worship begins! At that time the lead guitarist falls out, on the floor, I thought "OH NO! Here we go, I sneaked a looked at the Pastors and they are just enjoying it, then the bass and rhythm guitars players fall out followed by the drummer! It seems like after they got up we went on just like nothing happened. During the week talking with the visiting youth leader he said he was happy that his kids got to see a Holy Ghost experience. They returned several times with their parents.

Our attendance fluctuated for several years. The Lighthouse Christian Center began having satellite services from around the country. Then we began a Christian School, New Hope Christian School. They continued serving the people for several years till they answered a call to Pastor a church in Fort Davis, Texas.

Charles had married Ina Rose and had a successful family, with five step children, grand children and greatgrands, and a full ministry life. Not many people are aware of the difficulty in the early years. They gathered things up and attended and graduated from Bible school and came home, "No prophet is honored in his home town", and even Jesus family thought he had lost it. But their faith and belief in a God of love that would never fail them carried them through. Even some of his closes families were his greatest critics. Even when he was 700 more or less miles from home they had something to say.

Their continued faith in God would carry them through. Being close to him I saw the attacks and persecutions they endured. Especially, when he gave up his salary to support a school/church program and seemed never to flinch. He put in his job application several places with no success. He never seemed to answer his critics except with silence. Anyway over the years I never heard him!

Those years built their character and strengthened their understanding that no matter what the world calls facts or truth, they continued to stand on the Truth of the Word of God, "Let God be True and every man a liar."(Rn3:4NKJV) "If God be for you who can be against you!"(Num14:9;Rm8:31NKJV) Does this mean they had no problems, as a wise man said once, every garden has it's snake!" I'm sure they did. Charles has gone on to be with his Lord battling all the way to the end. Ina is at this time in Stillwater, OK overseeing the operation of Charles Koch Ministry. She is writing a weekly teaching and involved in intercessory prayer. She is Licensed and Ordained through Rhema Bible in Broken Arrow, OK.

I was married Jan. 3, 1993; I seldom speak of this season of life. I had prayed, begged and even tried bartering with God for a woman who would have a <u>Cracked Egg</u>! It seemed like a nurse, skilled in the compassion of care and tender loving care was what I needed. She seemed like a perfect fix, attractive, to me anyway, blonde most of the time. She had two small boys who needed a father image, and I met her in church and she was committed to prayer, worship, and bible study and heard from the Holy Spirit.

What didn't actually come out was her critical controlling spirit and she had difficulty with men in authority; including her dad who was a Vice-President of Pennzoil. The boys were dysfunctional and confused by lies they had been told. The oldest, 10yrs., was functioning at a 1st grade level while in the third grade. After the divorce, when they moved a year later he was at a fourth grade level in the fourth grade in all subjects. The younger was seemly at his grade level. I know it takes two; I gave it my best but when the credit cards were maxed and all savings gone, and no job. Well, she found her a married man and left for Texas. I hope this says all that needs to be said. That chapter of life is now closed!

I would not mind finding another and try it again! Please, only nice single women need to apply! We were divorced in Nov. 1993, lost home, car, almost all cloths, furniture, money, all credit cards maxed out and no job. But God is Good!

Went to work as a temporary employee at a convenience store on the interstate and worked there until Social Security began. Swept and mopped floors and waited on the customers, mostly truck drivers. It was strange at times when they looked at me and you could see on their face the look of how is he gonna give me my change. Not to mention watching me operate the credit card machine.

A mop handle broke one evening and embarrassingly I said "man how did that happen!" Joanie said, "Look your hooks wore the wood handle so thin it broke!!" Strange as it seems, she was right. We remain friends to this day. I got tired of cleaning the restrooms after the truckers and men who needed target practice. I told the new manager, why am I doing this, I'm on Social Security and don't need this abuse.

So I turned in my two week notice and left happy that I did everything I was asked to do and more, left content!! I have told people that I'm like a 55 Chevy, in good shape, with some missing parts, but I'm still a classic!

Around this time before the divorce several folks tried their best to help. One old friend Leroy would take me out to eat or to the grocery store and buy some groceries. He also helped to get some much need under clothes. All my clothes went the way of the trash I suppose. Had only a pair of ill fitting slip on shoes and two changes of summer clothes in the start of winter.

A local church bought me a microwave. On one day the X-wife brought by couple bags of groceries she said to help. The next day I went to the store and the assistant manager, who was a personal friend, showed me a returned check she had written for the two bags of groceries and ask if I would pick it up. "Eddie, I'm sorry" I said, "we are no longer together and that would be her responsibility." One older lady of another church attempted to help get me a suitable housing. A family offered me their older house they were remodeling, but they had moved to the country and they let me live there free. I was able to keep the lights on and talk the gas company to turn the gas back on without paying the arrears bill by previous occupant.

Lately I was speaking to a friend and her acquaintance and was asked how things were going. "Good, God is taking good care of me." She asked, "Do you have enough to get through the month?" My reply, "No, but I always seems to have just enough for the whole month!" Her friend replied. "Me, too! I always make it." Since that profession of faith, I now have help with house cleaning, meals, and people I'd never met before, offering to help. In thinking about that, the blessings came; I did not ask or demand them! If you are wondering, it's because He loves me!

Don't Try - Just Do

My sister gave me a picture of a oak tree once with a caption, "Even the mighty oak tree was once a nut!" My vision, may this nut become a mighty oak tree! We are told 'life' can be tough, and the tough get going. Or, you can have life, and have it to its fullest. Some try to do things and fail, not all but most, cause when you try you have begun by admitting you're going to fail. I've learned to always do my best at everything, even though I might not have reached the ultimate goal, there is still a goal, and I did accomplish what I set out to do. Most times like Edison, who did 10,000 experiments before he developed the light bulb. I've done things over and over each time knowing that success is not always in the first, but got better with each time I did it.

When I started cooking it got better each time, in my opinion. Trying with hooks to crack eggs to cook with water pump pliers! No, just do it, even if it means you have to pick out pieces before you cook them. Like those before me I would slice up potatoes with a steak knife, as thin as possible and fry them!

When I began shaving with hooks, it started with a razor, then an electric razor. Now I'm back to using a double edge safety razor. Now I still drop the razor, but if it drops on the floor like my electric razor, it doesn't break into three pieces or get baptized or drowned in the commode. Do I still nick myself, yes, but that's not a failure, it's just tough!

I can remember the first hamburger from the Dairy Queen, you know, the greasy ones with everything on it kind, the hickory smoked burger with sautéed onions! It looked good smelled good so we unwrapped it about halfway, and proceeded to pick it up to enjoy! Oh my! I picked it up and took that first bite, while chewing I looked down and the bun and meat had laid over the hooks and all the onions and other vegetables were running down the hook and all over everything. I could have quit eating hamburgers that day. Nope there was a fork available, but since that day I've learned with practice, usually at home before public, to overcome that and eat one in public.

Now sometimes it looks like a child or maybe even two sit where I sit! Sometimes I wear as much on me as in me, but changing clothes will correct that or a wash cloth! Yes it can be embarrassing, but that's just temporary and you'll live. I mentioned the most asked question from men earlier.

How do you, you know when you go to, you know. My reply, "Yes, very carefully!"

I was at the barber shop talking to my friend when nature called, he was busy cutting hair and talking so I ask, "Jack, okay if I use your little boy's room?" "Sure go ahead." as he pointed to the back. Well went through the door and entered the door to the room and reached for the light switch, remember (I'm blind in the dark). Couldn't find the switch with the hook, not wanting to scratch the wall, I tried to find it with my elbow, no such luck. The situation now is beginning to get urgent. I went back inside and ask, "Where's the switch?" Jack answered, "There's a string switch in the middle of the room." Well back into the little room trying to find the string, situation urgent, finally found it by bumping into it with my head, pulled the string. Not at this time, but there are situations where modern toilet paper dispensers can cause a difficulty. That's the second most asked question by men. Same answer, very carefully! Had a button hook to button my shirts, but learned how to slip those over my head like a pull over then leave the last one or two buttons left to button.

Where I eat here in small town America the cafe folks will cut my meat and hot cakes for me. It has been said that I'm just a little bit spoiled! I went for breakfast one morning at the "old" Depot Cafe, by the tracks, it was full and the only seat was at a large round table. There sit one of the men of the community sitting alone, a man of rough reputation. No other place so I sit there hoping nothing profane would be directed my way. I ordered my usual, flap jack and crispy bacon. The food came and the man says, "Can I help you with that?" Someday I'll learn not to judge a man or women by their reputation. I said, "Sure man," sliding the plate over, he cut up the pancake and put the syrup on. We carried on small talk with no profanity.

We believers are told we are in the world, not of it! We are supposed to be different! With God all things are possible!(Matt.19:26NKJV) And all things are possible to him who can believe! That's why we were told to have faith in "God!"

Some would say it was a Job testing, well I lived in a small trailer, then a house with lots of problems. No air conditioners, screens or phone. Went on unemployment, began working at a convenience store until began receiving Social Security Disability in 1994. Around this time my prosthesis were getting old and worn out. In fact they were held together with duct tape and rubber bands. Made contact with Oklahoma Department of Rehabilitation. They helped me get a new set. Amazingly they had me go to the world's best in prosthetics. Scott Sabolich Prosthesis and Research in OKC. One day at Sabolich's I was talking with a client who had a seizure and lost both arms as he fell into a vat of boiling oil at a chip company. He later died crossing a freeway in LA on his way to be interviewed on the Tonight Show! As we were talking and impressing one another, Scott the owner walks by and made comments about the arms and said "Except for Larry. When he came in his arms looked like they had been drug behind a 34 Chevy for miles!"

He was right! While there I have made some lifelong friends and acquaintances. Marc Ridgley a Prosthetist and Upper Extremity Specialist at Sabolich has been a life saver at times, well most times. He always listened and did his best to accommodate and fix my arms.

When a cable or strap breaks it can be a panic or just a nervous time. If I'm at the house and I have a spare set of arms, well it is only a manner of getting my shirt off which can be a trial and test, and put on the old set. It' can be a nervous time because you never know if they'll work or that they have been in storage might not work!

Sometimes I have called a relative and we have tried to rebuild them to where they'll work until I get to the shop. There has been times I driven myself to OKC with malfunctioning arms. Sometimes a sense of humor helps relieve the tension. Like I'll say, "I broke my arm, but its okay we tied it together with a shoe string and it don't hurt!" Which I have done! Sometimes I got to say see you later my arm is broke. We won't discuss what happens when you're in the bathroom when it breaks.

Remembering I visited the Pastor's house for a meeting and used his bathroom, well the door knob was a round knob, so I tapped on the door several times before they figured out what was up. If you're wondering, yes they let me out!

I moved into an apartment complex in late 1994. A outreach worker approached me to deliver a meal to a neighbor who was home bound. She asked me to deliver a meal to him and bring one for me also. Don, who became a friend, had a serious condition that wasn't always as bad as he made it out to be.

That began my service as a volunteer for Wheatheart Nutrition Center. It went from delivering one meal a day up to fourteen at a time daily, five days a week. For a period of approximately nine to ten months I drove their van delivering meals and transporting congregates to and from the site. Around 1997 I was named the Oklahoma DHS Volunteer of the Year award for my service. We received certificates from the Governor and State Legislature. My neighbor Don was a card. He had no phone so he would ask me to call people for him. I was being interviewed by Nancy Holden rehab counselor in preparation of them buying me a new set of arms, in burst Don through the back door, huffing and puffing shouting "call a ambulance Larry I'm having a heart attack!" After I called he left and said he'd wait in his apartment. I excused myself and told Mrs. Holden I'd be right back. They picked him up and took him to the hospital. Then we finished our business and she left.

Don called about a hour later and asked me to call his daughter and say, "Don has been admitted to the hospital, and he doesn't know how bad it is. Please come." He was home in three days. That was a common occurrence that happened regularly. Don had been a school mate of my Uncle Phil in high school. They had messed around together and played football together. I don't know if everything he told me was absolutely true about Uncle Phil cause when I repeated a story at a family reunion, I thought my aunts were going to excommunicate me!

Speaking of the family reunions, not sure of which holiday or special moments, we met on each holiday, Grandparents birthday, anniversaries, and other special days. We were double related; my Mother's husband's sister married my Mother's brother! I remember asking my Grandmother why my Uncle Larkin was at the Koch reunion and the Kirtley reunion, but she never was at the other Grandma's. Bless her heart, she did try to explain.

It seemed like as kids we were at a family gathering all the time. My aunts were all wonderful cooks! Every once in awhile a uncle would say, "Leave some deserts for us adults." He wasn't being mean; I would get a couple things of real food and also desert on the same plate. My reputation preceded me that I would reload with desserts before the adults were finished with their real food. It was a reputation well deserved. It was a special day when we had desert other than Gold Spot ice milk. I'm not complaining, just saying!

My cousin Ruth Ellen would be outside playing. That was when children played outside. We would play like we were adults back then. I told her that the husband was always older and bigger than the wife. Ellen informed me that wasn't always the case.

When visiting my Grandma Koch I would go out and lay in my grandma's peach and cherry trees and eat the fruit. When the peach tree was with fruit and I was finished eating and have climb down, I'd itch all over from peach fuzz. I never broke a branch! She also had a small garden pond, to my understanding that my dad built, with a black walnut tree. I never got the knack of opening a black walnut. Left a junky taste in my mouth when I would use my teeth to grind out the meat after breaking them with a rock on a rock!

There was a time when I'd go somewhere a family member would go just in case I had some sort of problem. When over at my sisters in Stillwater I would try to leave so I could reach home while the sun was still up. That was a joke around her house.

My oldest sister Marian, is widowed and works for OSU in the library in the government documents floor and has been recognized for her displays. She worked for the FBI in Washington D.C. She left Perry straight out of High School and transferred back to OKC to help with the family when dad left. She proofread some of this and said I hid lots of things from her. I pled the fifth.

She was sent to Texas to spent some time assisting the agents in Dallas who investigated President Kennedy's assassination. Then transferred to Springfield Illinois where she married and began her life as home maker and mother of two. Later they moved to Perkins, Oklahoma and she began her career with OSU. At this time she has two grandchildren. Not to mention a great help to yours truly.

One afternoon on the way to her house I had a flat tire. The highway SH-51 is always busy with commuters and college students. I surveyed the situation opening the trunk checking the spare and making sure the jack was there! Upon examination of the tire I found I couldn't handle the problem. I decided to wave down someone. Several waved back. It might of looked like I'm waving a weapon of some sort.

After about ten minutes a pick up stopped. They asked if they could help. They started to get the stuff out of the trunk when one said, "We will let the lawyer change it, he doesn't do any hard work all day." They would not tell me who they were only that they were 2 doctors and a lawyer on their way to a Oklahoma State basketball game.

After that day I began making plans to get a cell phone in case it happened somewhere remote. I was explaining to my Pastor what happened and that I was planning to get a cell phone. Call it insurance! A older lady heard me say that I was going to get a cell phone. She said, "Larry I thought you were a man of faith!" "Yes mam, but not a stupid one!" Two weeks later I discovered even she had got one!

Chaplain Years

Now I'm not telling or writing the history of "Overcomes Through The Crisis". It is well documented in other sources or you can call, Info, Perry, OK and get their office. This section is how it applied to my life.

In 1999 I began helping with a drug & alcohol recovery program and eventually was employed by them from about 2000 till 2008. During which time I served as chaplain and counseled our clients in the outpatient program and in patients at the recovery ranch. I also was a board of director's and bible instructor with them.

O.T.T.C. was one of those unexpected pleasures that the Holy Spirit sorta sneaks up on you and blesses and changes your life at the same time. Overcomes Through The Crisis is a Faith based recovery ministry.

When my good friend (Steven Gleason) had the vision, it was Overcomes Through The Cross, but he had to change the name to meet government concerns. He joined with Dr.

Lonnie Rutherford, local Pastor, to incorporate the ministry. They began to bring in officers to serve on the board. The ministry really began to form when he developed a home bible study in a board members (later) house. There were at times 14 to 18 men and women of all sort of issues and stages of despair. Alcoholics, I.V. Drug users, behavioral troubles and pot heads, crack heads and meth users. Some were involved in them all.

One evening, as we had scripture and a teaching, the group was asked to talk about their issues and what they wished to become of themselves. To my amazement (shouldn't of amazed me,) but all 14 had been divorced, including everyone else except Steven. Almost everyone wanted to be restored. Well not me. Just listening to their pain of rejection, I could feel that pain. Most had sunk to a low so deep they began blaming God or anyone else that seemed available at the time.

When will we ever learn, my opinion, we've been given a free moral will and when it's not made according to God's will, we blame Him or someone other than ourselves. I've never really discussed this with anyone that I know of. Now why was I there? I asked Steven one morning at the Depot Cafe, "why", he said, "if there are any questions you can give us the answer and keep us in line."

It seems to me that the ministry was having some effects in the community. These people now were in churches and in peer groups. They were required in a sense to attend church on Sunday morning.

Steve came to me and wanted to get a building for OTTC to meet in. There was a building next to the church so I pointed it out. After some prayer, he wanted to know how to claim it. He and a "old" experienced Christian like me, ha, "get some oil and we'll anoint it and claim it for the work of God!"

We anointed every corner, window, door and porch post including the boundaries and its corners for the ministry and favor of God to bring in or make it possible to secure the building. Not sure how much oil we placed or rubbed in, but it worked and the building became OTTC's official office and meeting room.

When Steve returned from the Philippines, troubles came from everywhere. One evening after bible study I bounced over to the office to talk with him, didn't realize he was living there, about starting a Thursday night prayer time, or whatever day he wanted.

There he was, busted, broken and pierced through. He did start the prayer and study group, but it didn't seem to progress. Then he moved into a house on Elm Street, became known as the devil's worst Nightmare on Elm Street. Lots of prayer, study, personal instruction, heartbreaks and life changing moments occurred there.

They began doing out sourcing for different companies doing packaging and cleaning items to be reclaimed. Steven wanted a time of spiritual reflection at the work site. My thoughts and they might be right or wrong, he wanted a local preacher come out each day and do a teaching. One day my cell phone rings, and he wants me to come out each day at 11:30 or so. He asked me to do a life changing message and began giving me what some of the people needed to hear and get decisions he wanted them to make. I stopped him and said something like this, "Steven, I am not a teacher but I will come and share with them whatever the Holy Spirit leads me to present and leave the rest up to the Spirit!"

That began my ministry as Chaplain and office clerk with the OTTC. Are there stories that go with that, yes sir, but that's another book, ha ha. I'll let Steven help write that one. Cause there were lots of joy, laughter, tears, oh the tears and heart breaks.

That's when the Thursday night prayer turned things the ministries way. One evening, as we were praying, don't remember everything that happened that night, Steven does, cause he journals, but as I remember it, Steven and I, with Maurice, began to call in financial favor, now I know some of you will have trouble with that, but that's why he had Maurice and I praying and not you. We no longer had said amen, and the phone rang, yep you guessed it, a "great big financial blessing came our way!" Well they started the ranch and a coffee shop and sowed into other ministries, including into Vietnam.

During this time a man who became a good friend that had converted from drug IV use to doing his best to live for God, was at church when he remembered something he wanted to give the pastor. So he and the Pastor went to his house before church. On the way talking and hands flying as he talked he went through a red light without stopping.

A policeman who knew him before his conversion stopped him. Now he had been testifying to all he knew that he was now clean. Here he is hand cuffed in broad daylight at one of the busiest intersection in town. Cops searching his car, he asking the officer to understand he was clean and that his Pastor was with him and all the people he had testified to where looking. And he asked him to remove the cuffs he was not going do anything. Nope the officer took him to jail tightening the cuffs. As they were putting him in the cell he was upset that he wouldn't loosen the cuffs. Mad he spoke some things to man and God about his painful wrists. He said he heard the Holy Spirit say, "Larry wishes he had a wrist to hurt!" He repented and later that day bailed out. It was the first time he can remember anyone being bailed out early Sunday afternoon!

Other than the fore mentioned Charles, Larry's siblings are; Clarence, Jr. has had a successful career in law enforcement, Federal, County and City. He retired from a local manufacturing company. He has been a tower of strength to his 3 children and 6 grandchildren. The youngest

Randy William, my name sake, died young! I'm sure, he and Jean, his wife of 48 years, are eagerly waiting great grandbaby footsteps! Clarence and Jean have been active in their church and have many young adults and teens who consider them as a spiritual and parental influence in their lives. He is still active today and works at different jobs.

My oldest sister Marian, is widowed and works for OSU in the library in the Government Documents Department. She has been recognized for her displays for the library. Marian worked for the FBI in Washington D.C. where she went immediately after graduating Perry High School. She later transferred to OKC to help with the family when our Mom and Dad divorced. She proofread what you are now reading and said I had kept lots of things from her. I plead the fifth.

She was sent to Dallas, TX. Field Office where the assassination of JFK was. She later transferred to the Springfield, Ill., field office where she met and married her husband and began her life as a home maker and mother of two. In 1979 they moved to Stillwater, OK. In 1984 she began her career with OSU at the Edmon Low Library. At this time she has two granddaughters. One in Florida will graduate from college in the Spring of 2012. The other is in grade school in Stillwater. I occasionally watch her house and dog and she keeps my hair cut and toes trimmed.

The youngest sister Nancy is married and mother of two and one "**great**" grand baby! She and I have always been close. She lived with me several years, well; put up with me is more like it. We watched after mother for years together, until she married. With her and her husband we helped Charles start his and Ina's church, along with others, including Ina's family. Nancy has worked as a bank teller since graduating high school. She had a break when she managed the Christian Book store we started. She helped start the first Operation Blessing in Perry. She blessed me many times in many ways!

Who Am I

Me? I was one of those guys that was not sold on myself. It never bothered me to come in second or last. Didn't like last, but when there are 10 in the race, only one can finish first. Why persecute a child for doing their best because they didn't meet "your" standard of success. Or insist your child live out your dreams.

It always seemed if I did my best, I was satisfied with it, if and when, I did my best. People would want me to do things with them. I told them sometimes, if I want to, okay, if I don't, well that's just to bad. I am who I am. One high school friend told me once, "Larry, I like you because when we ask you what you want to do, you just say, I don't know, what do you want to do." I think when I ran into these life problems, it never caused me to lose strength or a sense of purpose. I might get agitated but never got down on myself just because I failed to accomplish the plan or felt like a failure in the sight of others.

When the real God showed up, now He was never missing in action, and I was not where others or a organization said I should be, I seemed to know all God expected of me was as much as I understood of Him and His way. Sometimes it was kinda funny and I would find myself laughing at myself and it seemed He was laughing too. Like the day when I was so broke, busted and disgusted, praying I said something like, "GOD! It ain't fair here I am broke and you have streets of gold, the least; You could do is sweep me some dust! It's just not fair!!" I heard this, "It's mine." I began laughing repeating, "Yes it's Yours and You can do whatever with it You want." I didn't hear an audible voice, but an inner voice.

Laughter is like unto a medicine. Sometimes we are expecting a serious answer when a short correct one is all that is needed, **because your spirit will interpret the word given.** That is probably the reason I've been able to live and not commit suicide. I've always been a fellow who will roll with the punches and live with life's little situation and life's big problems.

I have a God who is Good. He said he came so I could have life and life more abundant. If it's the other, then I know it's not from Him, and if I wait, the season will change. He said if you're willing and obedient you'll eat the good of the land. Sometimes we're willing, but not so obedient and sometimes obedient and not so willing. Relax, as my brother would say, hey! It'll only hurt for a while! The prize is worth the wait!

It has never been about us, but seeking His Kingdom and being Right with Him.(Matt.6:33NKJV) It doesn't seem fair to the world, but it works! Just taking it easy one day at a time. Don't sweat the small stuff! I've started to hear the saying "don't pray for patience because He will teach you patience by giving you troubles.

After several years of declaring that myself, I was studying the Word and discovered patience is a fruit of the Spirit. Also in 1 Corinthians 13 it says love is patient (long-suffering in the Greek) and kind! God is Love! Patience is a fruit! It's developed or grown by being fed the Word and praying the Word and practicing the 'love' walk. Yes. Learning to lean or trust God in times of troubles will produce patience and character. But, being led by the Spirit will produce or birth patience.

Sometimes my patience drives microwave people bananas! One day while working for ODOT a supervisor comes into the lobby with an individual and said, "stay here until your brother gets off work. You can't wait in the work place!" I never thought anything of it until he started to talk and talk about himself and his marvelous truck driving ability. He kept talking and wanting me to acknowledge him and his abundant wisdom covering all subjects of life.

Man, I was happy when Phoebe came to give me my break. I flew out of the lobby headed to the break room.

While there I had a idea he would follow me so out the back hallway door I went, with no coffee. I walked down the end of the hall way to look into lobby area to see if he was there. Nope, he had left. After killing my 15 minute break in the hall way and of course the bath room, back to the lobby I went. Walking slowly and hoping he would be gone, well low and behold, he was gone! Asked Phoebe where he was? She said, "I told him to get a cup of coffee with you. He came back and said he couldn't find you. So I told him he would have to leave because he couldn't wait here all day!" He said "okay" and walked out the door!" Now why didn't I think of that! You can tell she had been a mother of five!

Later I asked, "GOD! Why did I have to undergo that agony?" His reply, "Larry, you have to love the ugly too!" I'm personally happy He listens to the ugly, aren't you?

My brother Charles was a person of great patience, people would say, "What are we going to do, Pastor!" He would shrug those shoulders; roll the eyes and say, "Trust God." I have a personality a lot like that. In my early years as a Believer I'd just receive instructions or complaints about my calm appearance interpreted as uncaring or not being responsible. What are you going to do about that? Nothing, just wait, it'll be okay. Must admit I'm a whole lot more talkative now than what I used to be.

One December after helping with Thanksgiving baskets and my own special gifts all I had left between me and the end of the month was three dollars. A several days before Christmas having a loaf of bread and a jar of peanut butter, I decided to go to the cafe and eat something.

I ordered the hot cake and bacon, as usual, Twana the waitress, brought it out cut up. When I asked for the ticket she said "O Lar it has been taken care of!" I never could spend that three dollars. Now, I knew every Christmas and my Birthday food was sent home with me and some birthday money usually came in. And it did, not sure from where, but this I know, God is Good and He is Faithful!

Pastor Jim McCool and I would go visiting people together. We would know at times that the individual need was cash. So we would put all our cash together before we went in and gave it to them in the name of the Church. My faith was good, but you need to understand, Jim had a wife and four children at home. My thought, I had no wife or children to ask me what are we going to do! His faith was a extremely compassionate special Pastors heart. And still is to this date!

Sometimes I'd buy food, not just staples, which I did, but fruits, nuts, candy bars and cookies and things that several food banks don't supply. But I always wanted the children's desires met, too!

I did at times try to defend God. I learned after several attempts of being God's greatest hero, a David, for modern times, He was able to defend Himself! I will defend the

Gospel of the Kingdom of God and the Word when instructed too!

I've found if you let people, maybe not all, vent or pour out their soul, they will most times answer their own question. Not only that, but Jesus said it's what's in a man's heart that comes out his mouth. Listen, listen, ask questions and keep my mouth shut and listen and it will come out, then, minister if appropriate! You're not the answer, but if you are a Spirit filled Believer, you've got the answer in you, if you listen and answer according to the Word.

I can understand what Paul was talking about. In the last days there will be a church that has the form of godliness, but denies the power thereof! Always wondered who'd be dumb enough to go to a church like that! How did a man that lived in the First century know about me? I mean I always, in church public, was a nice young man with manners, except in the other arenas of life. I knew John 3:16, parts of Mark 11:23 and was familiar with the 23rd Psalms. Wasn't that enough?

After all, my grandmas and great grandmas were Christian, and Grandpa was a Pentecostal Holiness. If Peter would let any grandchild in, it would be me. Then my sister in law spoiled the works, "Larry, God doesn't have grandchildren, just children!"

Just speaking my opinion having traveled and ministered at several churches and states, a church without the sound of children making noise and being children is a dying church! Yes as I said before, I believe in discipline, but the Bible says, spare not the rod, but don't **offend** the child!

I had the form of godliness, and not only denied the power there of, The Holy Spirit, but didn't think it was necessary. I was asked one day "Larry, how do you know that you're a Christian?" "Well" I said " That's what is written on the outside of the church!" Larry, do you speak in tongues? "Why yes, English!" It seemed funny then!

An Encouragement

I encourage you to keep looking and searching until you find the real Jesus. My life has not been the same. Though things I used to think were important are now fallen off of me and don't hold me back. I made a conscious and spoken out loud choice to change. Yes, I gave a voice to the choice to change. I decided to chose "Life" not what the world calls life, but life more abundantly. That God speaks. Invite Him in and choose life today. As you put Him, the Word, in your heart, then he said, "If My word abides in you and you abide in Me, **then**, you shall know the truth, and the truth shall set **you free!**" A easy walk, no, but worth every effort!

Life as a believer has not been a boring life, in fact there are times it has been real exciting and I've seen things occur that people say don't happen anymore! Not to mention even more fun! After several years, a young woman named Mary came to me and said something like would you be my best friend like you are Steven's best friend. I think I said okay.

Later she came back and asked me to pray for her broken toe, I said "The preacher is up front. He'd be happy to, or even your friend Steven. She said no, you. Well, up to the front we went, got the preacher and Steven to help. She stuck the foot out; we had her put it on the chair. Man, that toe had been stepped on and was swollen up like a big green grape sticking straight out to the side, no wonder she couldn't wear regular shoes. I prayed, declared and decreed it healed and charged it to return to the normal position God created it to be in. Oh! My! Right in front of our eyes, the swelling went down; the toe did a right turn and repositioned itself where it was supposed to be. Later, that opened the door for Jesus to baptize her in the Holy Spirit. Even today when I need a special person to believe with me in prayer, Mary is the one I call!

I eat at a nutrition site operated by government agencies. We were waiting for the meal to be brought out and served. The outreach worker came in a began telling the seniors that grant monies given to the agency was still available but only for a short time. Also the money was now limited. She was explaining it was for whatever need they had such as dental work. Listening I thought man that would be a answer to prayer. To my surprise and the outreach worker, nobody but one little woman responded. So I asked if I could apply. She asked, How old are you? What is your source of income? What is your birthday?"

Then she wanted to know what my problem was? When I told her she said, "I do not think they will pay or spend that much on you, Larry. But I will submit the request. Two weeks later my phone rings, and a pleasant voice says, "This is Doctor Anderson's office, when would you like your first appointment." In my wisdom I said, "What?" She repeated herself and I said, "Can I call you back?" She replied, "I will call you again in two days."

I had not received any info that I had been approved. So I went to see the outreach worker who said, "Who told you had been approved?" Well no one except the Doctor's office. After a few moments of searching and calling we found out that a full set of dental work had been approved.

When at the office the dentist came in and said, "What do you want us to do?" I responded "Fix the old set." He looked and said, "What will the agency pay for?" I shrugged my shoulders. The office clerk came in and said, "They will pay for everything we do." The dentist asked her to confirm that!" She came back and confirmed information. God supplied probably a three thousand six hundred dollars or more of dental work! As I walked out of the office after five months of work, the office clerk said, "Paid in full, see you Larry!"

Angels are a subject I've thought about for years, ever since all the silly shows that's been on TV and Hollywood's versions. I know I heard the bible stories about them and their adventures. I pray that you have taken time to ask the Holy Spirit to help you understand the purpose and His intent as He leads me in this adventure. The angel Clarence in The Christmas Story, was a movie that got me interested in the study of angels. I understand that was entertainment and not scriptural. But after an experience at work, a co-worker asked me a question to do with our beliefs; we attended the same church for years. Now she was like I used to be, attended regularly, never missed an Easter or Christmas. I responded to her question with scripture. She replied, "Oh I don't read much religious stuff, whatever people say is what I believe and you know God said, in Oh God the movie," and proceeded to quote George Burns. But that was Hollywood, girl. "Yes" she replied, "but it sounded good to me."

In trying to understand angels I've struggled with reading several books. After that I've studied the biblical accounts which are many and quite awesome!

My mother slept in the bedroom across the hall. She was having some issues and I prayed for protection for her. There were times I'd awake to find her starting to go out the front door. One night about 11:30 or there about, I was awakened by her saying, "Larry, Larry!" Startled I think I said, "What?" Her reply, "Who are these men dressed in white doing in my bedroom". "Oh, mother they're angels there to help you." She said, "Oh, okay." She went back to bed and I slept sound thereafter.

It wasn't always that way. There was the evening I woke up and fear was heavy in the house. I managed to get up and stepped into mother's room; she was sleeping, but at the head of her bed was a dark angel outlined in fire with beady red fiery eyes of hate. You know when flesh meets spirit; flesh wants to crawl under the bed! It took some doing but I finally got the name of "JESUS" out. Softly at first then the name came out more boldly. It disappeared, to my relief!

As I turned to go back to my bedroom, there at the other end of the hall way he stood. Eyes ablaze and outlined in reddish orange flames on his legs and shoulders ablaze. I said, I think, "Rebuke you in Jesus name." It smiled and left.

Several days later while I was at church, mother decided she needed to walk home, she was at home. The wonderful people of Perry and my family searched everywhere for her in the city; on horseback, in cars with flash lights and in back of pickups. Several people took leave from their work to search for her, even blood hounds.

She was eventually found in a deep ditch next to the railroad. When we talked with her in the ER I asked her if the trains were loud. "OH! Yes!" Scratched from her head to toes, but okay! A Family member with her family was praying about her, one of the daughters said, something to the effect, there's a mask, or similar, on her and preventing her being discovered. They broke the assignment off her and within minutes she was discovered. Happenstance, not likely!

Angels were on assignment. I know that's a little difficult to believe, but it happened.

That's why I don't give any witchcraft any right to operate around me! My family has never heard these stories, so I'm like Paul; this is written with fear and trembling. I've had several visions and dreams of angels here at my home.

I have seen them standing in the room, kneeling by the bed. And they were once standing in pairs at the foot of the bed and three sets of two standing in the living room and a pair in the yard in front and two pairs on the roof.

I have seen them in parking lots and other locations. When I was where I was given chances to deliver the word; Angels would be in the meetings. Now they weren't seen, but they were felt, if you pardon that term.

One evening while preaching a angel dressed in woven clothes was standing by me. Why, because I needed all the confidence and help that was available, when needed! Also I think at times you feel vulnerable when go to bed without arms with concerns what would happen if an emergency would happen and not be able to get to the arms.

There has been times that I couldn't open a jar or a door knob of some sort, I would get a little radical and yell, yes I yell, He doesn't mind you being honest with Him, "God! I need help! Send an angel or someone!" You would be surprised how quick He has answered. One snow storm that snowed me in, I was trying to open a large jar of peanut butter, one of my staples, I shouted, "Jesus that's what I meant when I said I NEED A WIFE." Could not get that silly lid to budge! Well, He didn't send a wife, PTL, or even a single woman or a neighbor. One more try I thought, or I'll starve to death, the lid almost just fell off it was so loose.

I was told go home and cope with life! Thank God I have a wonderful family that helped me in every way possible. But I finally had to choose to live with it! An ill word spoken at a ill time produces an ill effect!

"Sticks and stones may break my bones, but words cannot hurt me!" Maybe the greatest destructive lie ever told from the pit! Who have we murdered or destroyed by our words spoken in haste or even in what we call corrective criticism or tough love! Yes there is a time for correction and applied discipline, but a soft answer turns away wrath. A good man is slow to speak!

Apostle Paul gave us theses thoughts that scripture are for; correction, instruction, reprove and rebuke. II Timothy 3:16 scripture is given by inspiration of God, and is profitable for doctrine, for reproof, <u>for correction, for instruction</u> in righteousness: II Timothy 4:2b,KJV) <u>reprove, rebuke, exhort with</u> <u>long suffering and doctrine.</u>

Choose right! Life is Good, God is Good, try good, and you will like it! Choose Life; get patience to live life to the fullest!

Larry's Accomplishments Member Perry City Council 1973; Member Board of Adjustments City of Perry 1976; Carter Delegate to the Democrat District Convention; Former member American Legion Perry OK.; Life Member VFW Post 1843 Glendale OK.;

Oklahoma Handicapped Citizen of the Year 1979; Oklahoma DHS Volunteer of the Year 1997;(1 of several) Board Member Charles Koch Ministry; License with World Ministry Fellowship; Former Member and Pass President Cherokee Strip Historical Society.

To make contact with Larry or
Schedule a meeting <u>kochlw43@gmail.com</u>